THE COMMUNITY COLLEGE :

VALUES & VISION & VITALITY

Edmund J. Gleazer, Jr.

Published with Support from
the Shell Companies Foundation, Incorporated
and the W. K. Kellogg Foundation

Copyright 1980

Price: $6.50

American Association of Community and
Junior Colleges/One Dupont Circle, N.W./
Washington, D.C. 20036

ISBN 0-87117-097-3

i

FOREWORD

It might be of interest to the reader and useful in appraisal of this book if I were to indicate briefly what I had in mind as I wrote. I began this venture with journeys to several states in early 1979 to find out what people were thinking about when they called for examination of "community college mission." Because state officials and legislators increasingly influence community college fortunes, I talked with many of them and am grateful for their cooperation. I visited several community colleges in six states to confer with trustees, presidents, faculty, students, community groups, and others associated with the colleges. In essence, my question to all parties was—"What do you consider to be the central elements in community college mission over the next several years?" Answers to that question helped to start me on this editorial path.

I have written this book for a number of reasons. In work which the Association is doing with assistance from the W. K. Kellogg Foundation, we are trying to identify a policy framework that will facilitate lifelong education. It seemed helpful to try to describe the kind of community college that would develop as a result of more favorable policies. Further, the AACJC is engaged in a planning process with respect to its own mission and objectives over the next several years. The book is available as a resource for that exercise. And probably most important, I had reached a point in my own career where I felt it would be rewarding to take the time and to experience the discipline required in expressing views that have grown out of more than 20 years of national experience in community college education.

Let me tell you what the book is not. It is not a "how-to-do-it" manual, although I hope the illustrations offered will be useful. It is not a commission report or a textbook. Instead, I look upon it as a series of essays.

An essay is usually written from a personal point of view and does not attempt completeness. That is a good description of my efforts. The community college field is vast; no publication such as this one can attempt to be comprehensive. Where I have used one illustration, 100 could have been drawn upon. Many interesting developments have been left out. There was no room for them. When I began writing, I had accumulated enough excellent materials to fill several file drawers. But after serious deliberation with myself, I decided to leave those materials where they were and to closet myself with a few hundred pages of good interview notes which I had scribbled on many a yellow tablet.

Others have written about specifics. My purpose is to suggest ideas of sufficient interest to people so that they may be inclined to develop them in their particular settings. It has not been my intent to fully elaborate the ideas or to go to great lengths in trying to document impressions. I leave it to others, or to myself at another time, to pursue in greater detail such perplexing problems as finance and control.

Last, this is not an "official" report of AACJC. I have the privilege of working for a Board of Directors which encourages creativity and initiative. These are not their words. However, in a sense they are responsible, for it has been the quality of association which I have had with these colleagues and others in our field which has stimulated and influenced my views.

Edmund J. Gleazer, Jr.
Washington, D.C., January, 1980

APPRECIATION

Many people have helped me during the year 1979 as this book matured. A few hundred busy people took the time to talk with me. Others helped with hospitality and travel arrangements. I am particularly grateful to Francis Pray and to AACJC staff members, among them Roger Yarrington, Jamison Gilder, William Harper, and not forgetting Mary Clayton who, after working with me for several years now, has surely become surfeited in notes, speeches, and airline tickets and through it all maintains her good humor.

EJG

CONTENTS

Chapter I

THE COMMUNITY COLLEGE—

WHAT IS IT?
WHAT IS IT FOR?

Developments in this country and abroad dwarf our pre-occupations with educational institutions as we move into the 1980's. In the face of these, why should I write about community colleges and why should you take the time to read what I have to say about them? Those of us who have special interests in schools or colleges may appear to be pleaders for those possessions we hold dear at a time that our way of life more than our possessions is in jeopardy.

The term ''jeopardy'' suggests ''danger'' and ''peril.'' That is not an overstatement. However, there is a positive factor as well. There are possibilities in this time of unparalleled change for a quality of life better than we have known if we can somehow nullify those things that threaten our way of life.

The point is that heated and even informed discussion about how to finance education, the ups and downs of college enrollments, and whether Johnnie can read when he graduates from high school cannot hold a candle to public interest in the fact that the dollar buys less each year, gasoline is harder and more costly to get, and nobody seems to have the answer to how we can get this nation "back to the stability of the good old days."

Education per se is not a high priority item on either the public's agenda or that of policy makers. That's too bad, for surely there are values in learning for learning's sake. The fact is, however, that if education is to capture public interest, it has to be education *for* something. Somehow the case needs to be made that education is of utility as related to that dollar problem, and the energy crisis, and the need for sense of purpose and direction in government.

The Fact of Change

As educators we have given our attention to patching the roofs of our structures, to more efficient heating and cooling, to improving the communication system, while developments outside our walls are washing away at the footings. The basic, inexorable, unmistakable fact and force to deal with is that of CHANGE—unparalleled and unprecedented change that perplexes the public, confounds the authorities, and demands response from education, one of its instigators. R. H. Dave talks about change in his book on lifelong education:

> The contemporary period of history is characterized by rapid and unprecedented change in practically all aspects of life. What A. N. Whitehead observed in the early thirties about the time-span of change and its impact on education has become more relevant in the seventies, and trends in many fields clearly suggest that his farsighted statement will apply even more as we move towards the year 2000 and beyond. Whitehead said:

> . . . in the past the time-span of important change was considerably longer than that of a single human life. Thus mankind was trained to adapt itself to fixed conditions.

> Today this time-span is considerably shorter than that of human life, and accordingly our training must prepare individuals to face a novelty of conditions.[1]

In the closing years of the 1970's, community colleges experienced a "novelty of conditions." The institutions are changing—they have changed from the earlier days of high school extension and the remarkable period of expansion and community orientation of the 1960's.

The institution that sought a campus and other paraphernalia of the collegiate ways often functions in multiple locations throughout its district, and chafes frequently in its collegiate harness, even to the point of declaring that the collegiate mode might be defeating its purposes.

The college that enrolled late adolescent high school graduates to prepare them for upper-division work in four-year colleges now preponderantly serves people well beyond their early twenties and high school graduation, if indeed they have been graduated.

Most of the participants in community college programs take a course or two while they work full-time or part-time. They are likely to be married and have children. And a majority are either preparing directly for employment or are trying to improve their job situations.

Another significant change has to do with financial support and control of the institution. While earlier, both control and support were predominantly local, now the state provides a majority of the money and has more to say about how it will be used.

And the state raises questions about community college services that do not fit the categories of transfer or occupational programs. Why should the college get support for recreational and avocational programs? What business does the college have in nursing homes? Should the state pay for non-credit programs? Why are so many community college students not interested in or at least not getting a degree, a certificate, a credential?

Of great concern to the states is the increase in dollars required of them from relatively modest amounts twenty years ago to a significant portion of their budgets as the institutions grew beyond most expectations and the proportion of state support became larger. No wonder that a spokesman for a legislative budget office asserted in the spring of 1979 that the state had reached a point where it had to have a say—and it had to ask what community colleges are and what are they actually doing.

Clearly the institutions have changed and continue to change. Questions are raised increasingly, in the face of taxpayer movements and inflation, as to whether these are justifiable directions of change. And for the policy makers, they ask, shall we validate these changes in legislation?

Newspaper editorials elaborate on the theme, saying it is time for a hard look at community colleges and their missions. And within the institutions themselves, rising costs, changes in enrollment mix, and harder-to-get tax dollars require examination of priorities. Tough questions confront college leadership, sometimes resulting in the ultimate question: For what are we willing to go to the barricades?

Trapped in Tradition

One of the first problems encountered in determining what the community college is and what it does is the terminology used to describe and define the institution. "We are trapped in the traditional view of college," assert more than a few community college leaders. Classrooms, credits, lectures, grades, semesters, professors, campuses, and students comprise the direction-determining baggage of an institution which seeks appropriate forms to match its functions.

Many terms have connotations that are more appropriate for traditional four-year colleges. During a transitional period this would be expected. Older terms often are used to describe new items because more appropriate terms have not been coined. McLuhan alerts us, for example, to a time when trains were called "iron horses," and automobiles were "horseless carriages," and radio was called "wireless." The time has come when the community college needs to be using its own terms, not those that connoted its beginnings.

Would it not be more appropriate, for example, to use the word "learner" rather than the word "student" for persons being served? Learner carries the spirit that anyone who wants to learn is invited, and that instructional emphasis is learner-centered. Much in the same way that libraries do not count their users as "students" and do not "graduate" their users, it is time to "internalize" the same relationship with community college learners—an ongoing, continuous relationship with participants who are greatly dissimilar in age, motivations, abilities, and interests.

Another possible candidate for more appropriate labeling is the term "college." Historically, the "two-year college" (two-year is a good example of inaccurate terminology for comparatively few students use the college for precisely two years) preferred "college" because the connotation helped them to achieve "status." It brought citizen understanding and support (everybody knows what a college is). And there is some prestige to identification with "higher education." That is the whole point. What was appropriate and helpful formerly is not likely to remain so in times of rapid and new kinds of changes. Hence, not surprisingly, a term which was helpful now needs to be reconsidered. It may get in the way of what really needs to be done in the community. However, unless a decidedly better term can be found, "community college," with accent on the first word, should continue to have utility.

Questions About Mission

We have one more brief encounter in the semantics thicket before probing the rudiments of community college mission. "Mission," in terms of goals and programs and objectives, may be the wrong or a misunderstood word. Characteristically, questions about college priorities often produce response in terms of programs—college transfer, occupational, or remediation. Program priorities have changed, no question about that. When new community college legislation was under consideration in Illinois in the early 1960's, the primary concern was "When your child is ready for college, will college be ready for him?" There was fear that there would not be room enough in the colleges for the youth coming out of the high schools. The community college was sold on the basis, primarily, of providing college space and, secondarily, vocational-technical training. "Mission," as far as the public was concerned, was "college." Now the community colleges of Illinois have shifted to a different order of emphasis. Does such change suggest that community college mission may be more a type of process than program?

The institutions are markedly different. People in the community colleges in Chicago wear different sweatshirts from those worn on Western Illinois campuses. There are different values and different political realities. The institutions serve unique communities and needs. Some observers say there are dangers in attempting to be specific with regard to mission:

> Anytime we can describe the community college in definitive, specific terms, we will destroy it. It has to change. It has to be different in different areas. You need to keep moving as a community college norm. We need to look at people but we tend to look at the institution. We should not try to push the river in a different direction.

Adaptability is one element in mission or process commonly agreed upon. The institution must be able to change as communities change with new conditions, demands, or circumstances. One of the paradoxes of the Proposition 13 syndrome may be a forced hardening of mission just when response should be most flexible and force the division of the turf among K–12, community colleges, and four-year institutions at a time when relationships based on best service should be encouraged most.

Community Awareness

That modifying word, "community," is achieving greater recognition and importance. No question about it. Members of a county legislative body say that the mission of the community college is to keep pace with the community and "help us make this county an attractive one in which to do business. If you do that, the college will be around a long time." The key element, say college spokesmen, is to be a community resource in cooperation with other community agencies.

A search was under way in one county for a president to succeed a man who was retiring after 20 years in the position. The board was somewhat affronted to have a candidate ask them what they thought the institution should become over the next 10 years. After the initial shock, the board agreed that the question was justified and that, in order to determine what the college should be, it was necessary to project developments in the county that sponsored the institution.

"Increased community awareness" is now a high priority objective frequently cited in institutional plans. "Services shall reflect the needs of those persons residing in the college service area," declares a state-level document in Michigan. An awareness of the needs of persons in the college area requires a stance unfortunately sometimes lacking in educators or provided for in institutional structures. One of the biggest problems facing education may be a reluctance (or inability) for people in education to relate on a regular basis with people in business, industry, the unions, and agriculture. A note sounded repeatedly as one talks with people about educational needs is that they perceive schools and colleges as "self-contained enclaves of educators."

At the same time the reverse is heard, conceivably signaling different days ahead. Some leaders say:

> Maybe now we'll get back to our job, to our real philosophy, that is, a total look at our community and to help it grow and prosper and to do this because we think it is right and not because of financial need but because we want to make this community a better one.

In probing community-college relationships, a number of

questions soon surface. Is the college role limited to response or reaction to community needs, pressures, and requests? Or are there not more sophisticated services appropriate to the identification and analysis of problems *and* proposed solutions? And further, should not the community college play a part in forecasting the shape of society to come, and leading its community to understand the coming changes, make provisions for coping with them, and providing services to meet them?

The concept of institutional mission conveys the notion of an organization which has purpose and functions and desired outcomes. There are conditions that facilitate and impede its functions. We have referred to three elements that are associated with viable community colleges. They have the capacity to be adaptable, they maintain a continuing relationship with learners, and they are community-oriented. Now another question must be raised. Of all possible learners in the community setting, are there some whose needs should be given precedence?

To Extend Opportunity

Although it may seem out of place to consult tradition when considering the effect of rapid change, it is worth recalling that community colleges and their progenitors, public junior colleges, were established to *extend* educational opportunity. People of limited financial means now had a low-cost institution available. For those who could not leave the community to go to college there was one within commuting distance. And those uncertain about their academic abilities or who wanted programs geared more quickly to employment than the four-year colleges offered found an environment responsive to those needs. Historically, the community college was based on the assumption that there were large numbers of people not served by existing institutions and the unserved were to be the clientele of these new colleges.

The leitmotif continues. The theme is sounded in numerous ways: Community colleges should reach out. Go to people who are unserved. Give priority to those who need the education they did not get at an earlier age. Serve the students with roots in their community and who have jobs there. Give those who need it a second chance. Bring people into the mainstream. Serve people handicapped by problems of cost and transportation.

These signposts suggest perimeters for those who fear the community college will attempt to be "all things to all people."

Priority is given to those whose educational options are limited by a variety of circumstances. Very few people will disagree with these institutional aims. They have the ring of social worth. However, the necessary conditions and results are not as easy to accept.

If the community college is to reach the unserved, initiatives are required. Availability of the college cannot be kept secret from those outside the primary communication networks in the community. We are told that the most significant obstacle to participation in adult learning activities is lack of information about such opportunities. Although legislators question community college recruitment efforts, equity is simply not possible unless those outside the conventional information systems are purposively sought.

A Variety of Learners

And there is the problem of diversity. An institution that focuses on the "unserved" will find many reasons for that circumstance. In fact, it might be assumed that the unserved are in that condition because other institutions find it not feasible, desirable, or profitable to respond to their needs. Therefore, substantial costs are likely to be incurred in fulfilling this aspect of the community college charter. Financial costs of dealing effectively with diversity. And costs, too, in terms of prestige, for in our existing academic value system an institution that invites those needing a second chance, and which gives priority to those of limited educational options, is not going to threaten the status of the Ivy League, a circumstance that may raise doubts among some members of the college family. Such institutions will have to establish prestige on bases quite different from those of the usual college ranking system. Although more difficult to make visible than conventional results, perhaps a way could be found to assign value in terms of the learning stimulated and the human potential released.

A careful observer of the community college scene is impressed by the remarkably broad spectrum of human beings to be found there. This comprehensive nature of the community college is an aspect of American education most difficult to interpret to visitors from abroad. And its apparent developing span prompts faculty within the institutions themselves to ask how much diversity can be accommodated within one organization.

As indicated earlier, although there are marked differences among institutions, in many there will be found recent high school graduates just beginning their college work on the one hand, and adults who already have college degrees on the other. There may be adults learning basic verbal and numeracy skills as well as those qualifying for a certificate of high school completion. A high proportion of learners is qualifying for job entry or to be upgraded in employment. Community forums involve large numbers of the citizenry in discussing such issues as taxation, energy, and health.

There may be off-campus centers for Indo-Chinese. English taught as a second language. Among the learners are perhaps some who have formed a not-for-profit corporation to rehabilitate housing. Under CETA programs, Chinese are qualifying in American cookery and learning English at the same time. And perhaps an "honors college" is organized for highly qualified students who are not able to go away to college.

Out of that mix arise a good many questions. Can we have both honors programs and remediation? Should we build our future on CETA? With growth in numbers of adults, do we give up youth? Can we afford to give some people more time to learn than others? Can we really bring them up to college level? Should we continue to be open to everyone or become more selective?

Although there is a tendency for many questions to be raised in program terms, the major issue seems to be that of whether diversity can be dealt with. The community college has a greater variety of participants than any other educational institution. There is really no question about that. The case has been made repeatedly for the advantages of having numerous program options available within a single institution for people who are undecided with respect to occupational and educational goals. Values in having a learning environment of people of different generations, ethnic backgrounds, and socio-economic characteristics have been cited, though not as frequently. Some selective institutions deliberately aim to avoid the dangers of homogeneity by their admission policies.

No such threat faces the community college. One is reminded of the question put to John Hannah, president of Michigan State University, some years ago. He was asked how large a university should be. And he replied in good Socratic manner: How large should a city be? Obviously, the answer is, that depends. That depends on what you expect of the city. And similarly, how much diversity can be accommodated depends—depends to a great extent on what that college is to do. If the central aim of the college is to involve the citizenry in learning activities that result in a better community, then the mixture of people involved can be beneficial. For this is a real world—a continuum from slow learners to fast. A world of different income levels and social interests—businessmen and farmers, young people and older, an ethnic and racial mosaic. This is the community at learning, not the groves of academe. There is no town and gown dichotomy and no need for simulation. Perhaps there is no better way to develop viable communities than to involve the citizens, as many as possible, in learning experiences where they can interact. The community college we envision provides that opportunity. It is more a process than a place. The learners are the same people we meet in the shops and offices and plants. They govern the city and install the telephones. They deliver the papers and repair the cars. Can this diversity be accommodated? If it can in the community, why not by the college? And if by the college, certainly by all odds in the community.

A Means of Connection

Now hold on, some of you may be saying. Do you see the community college domain as that of responding to the learning needs and interests of the whole city or community? You have proposed as a college aim the involvement of the citizenry in learning activities with the expectation that a better community will result. Isn't that a pretty tall order for a single educational institution, even one as broad-gauged as the community college? Obviously such concerns are justified. The college has neither the capacity nor the resources solely on its own to be the learning system for the entire community. Even beyond that, such an approach collides immediately with the elements of mission already proposed. However, the community college is uniquely qualified to become the *nexus* of a community learning system, relating organizations with educational functions into a complex sufficient to respond to the population's learning needs.

"Nexus" is defined as a "bond, link, or tie existing between members of a group, a means of connection between things." In almost any community there are organizations that provide opportunity for formal, non-formal, and informal learning activities. Among these are radio and television stations, newspapers, libraries, museums, schools, colleges, theaters, parks, orchestras, dance groups, unions, and clubs. An institution dedicated to the encouragement of learning is aware of the wealth of community resources available and utilizes such means as fully as possible. Granted that is true, what qualifies the community college to play a "nexus" role? What attributes prompt it to initiate "links" or "connections" among members of the learning system?

One example is found in the fact, as described earlier, that for many community college learners, education is concurrent with employment and civic activities. They participate in other organizations. They may be officers in unions or on library boards or members of a community dance group or orchestra. They are on the boards of the YMCA and the League of Women Voters and the Taxpayers League. A survey of community college "students" would find them identified with a multitude of voluntary associations that characterize American community life. In Scandinavia, the major popular associations encourage and sponsor adult learning activities with remarkable participation rates. Similar possibilities are open to the community college as it joins with those organizations for which it provides a common ground. Informal, personal relationships can lead to organizational ties.

There is another feature of these community institutions which aids the connecting process. A large number of faculty are active in the practice of their trade and profession as well as in their teaching. Sometimes referred to as "professor-practitioners," or adjunct professors, they work as real estate insurance brokers, lawyers, engineers, craftsmen, and doctors and provide further means for linking up with other parts of the community's learning system. Similar possibilities exist through numerous advisory committees to college programs as well as in the linkage established by use of "clinical" facilities in health, business, and industrial settings.

Through its vertical connections in the educational hierarchy and its horizontal relationships with other community agencies, the community college can literally be "the middle man." One would think that schools, community colleges, and universities would have the most natural of connections as learners move through them in the formal education process. All too often, though, that is not the case. Students seem obliged to jump from pool to pool rather than finding themselves in a continuing stream. In one state, where there has been a dramatic decline in achievement levels of secondary school students, the chairman of the state board of education pleads for cooperative activities between community colleges and the schools *before* the high school leavers apply for admission to community colleges. The self-interest of community colleges is certainly involved, for most of those students will be knocking on their doors. One would expect collaborative relations to be of the highest order among institutions that have in common community support, community governance, and community orientation, such as is true of the elementary and secondary schools, community schools, and community colleges.

In some states there is now a legislative mandate for such relationships, with cooperation and coordination as conditions for state funds. However, even without that pressure institutions of their own volition now cooperate in data processing, in sharing of facilities, and in establishing inter-institutional faculty teams. In a number of places community colleges also provide space for university programs and have worked out articulation agreements that are tantamount to assuring automatic transfer for qualified students.

Perhaps the strongest case for the nexus role of the community college rests upon its informational capabilities. If the college is to identify and analyze community problems and propose solutions, and if the college is to forecast the shape of society to come, and if the college is to identify and seek out those who have educational needs, and if the college is to have the knowledge of the community required to deal with diversity, then obviously the college must know its community and must have data that will project trends and developments.

Data collection is not accomplished by reading news releases. What is required is daily communication with the business community, the county and city planning bodies, employment agencies, research organizations, the chambers of commerce, state and federal agencies, school officials, census bureaus, and the media. Here's the point. The community college, in the very process of doing what it needs to do to function effectively, maintains relationships that qualify it to be a useful nexus for the community learning system.

A Search for Mission

We are on a search for a description of community college mission. For a variety of reasons many people want specific information about what the tasks of the institution are and what they ought to be. The interests of legislators have stepped up as funding for the colleges has increased. Beyond any doubt, the colleges are changing what they do. Twenty years ago most legislators apparently envisioned their roles as service to recent high school graduates who wanted a year or two of postsecondary schooling in the local community before taking a job or going on to the university. Now, as noted previously, the majority of students are part-time; they have already assumed responsibilities of job and family life. Many are there for programs or services that do not fit the arrangement of semesters and credits. A good deal of the work is not in a campus setting. An increasing number of learners have already received associate degrees and beyond. Under contract, services are provided in business and industry and governmental agencies. Courses are taken through radio and television and newspapers, with the possibility that the learner will not enter a college classroom, but will earn college credit. Learning activities are made available in nursing homes and condominiums, recreation centers, and correctional institutions. A hundred examples could be given of differences between the community college of 1980 and the college of 1965.

But what of the college through this decade of the 80's? Seldom has there been so much discussion in state capitals, and in the institutions themselves, about services the colleges should provide and, of course, who should pay for them. In these pages I have been looking for a sense of mission. For background, I questioned hundreds of policy makers, educational practitioners, and community people in a number of states about what the community college should be doing. The responses were varied. Frustration is often evident. Structures, physical facilities, existing policies, and even terminology are frequently perceived to constrict and to compel institutional behavior no longer appropriate to changed circumstances.

I asked what the institutions should do during the next ten years. I pressed for a sense of priorities and the responses came: We should work more closely with business and industry. There will be more adults. Older people will be served in larger numbers. With the requirements for competency tests in the secondary schools, one of our big jobs will be "remediation." We will work in partnership with other community agencies. A greater proportion of students will be in the technologies. The mission will be shaped by the legislature. We live in a changing world. Institutions ought to try to develop their own sense of mission and then make the case for resources for the people in the state capital. We need to be moving out to where the people are. We will serve more people but have fewer FTE's. Community colleges should work out their own approaches or they are just going to be another institution in a declining community of higher education. If the members of the community supporting the institution want these programs (leisure-type courses), we will provide them.

To Do or To Be

On the surface, there are few compelling threads of broad agreement, none strong enough to suggest that this or that is the community college mission. The thought begins to take form that perhaps the most important issue is not really what the community college is to do, but what it is to be. Clearly, change in our society is so rapid that what is required today may be an option, or even forgotten tomorrow. And what is not known today could be commonplace tomorrow. The communities that are now the context for community college operations are vastly different and the pace of change in them is uneven. The kind of resources available in community learning systems will be different. A statement of mission for institutions that covers such a variegated field must be general and not specific. It cannot be put in program terms and be useful for the community college as a whole.

So, of basic and prior importance to the concept of mission—what the institution is to do—is a description of what the institution will be. A useful and appropriate analogy can be found in an approach to suitable education for individuals in this world of change. "For the first time in history," writes Edgar Faure, "education is now engaged in preparing men for a type of society which does not yet exist." He continues:

> This presents educational systems with a task which is all the more novel in that the function of education down the ages has usually been to reproduce the contemporary society and existing social relationships . . . At a time when the mission of education should be to train "unknown children for an unknown world," the force of circumstances demands that educationists do some hard thinking, and that in so doing they shape the future.[2]

Faure's theme of dealing with change and the unknown is amplified with respect to preparing people for maximum vocational mobility.

> Educational action to prepare for work and active life should aim less at training young people to practice a given trade or profession than at equipping them to adapt themselves to a variety of jobs, at developing their capacities continuously, in order to keep pace with developing production methods and working conditions.[3]

So this notable report of UNESCO urges that we "no longer

assiduously acquire knowledge once and for all, but learn how to build a continually evolving body of knowledge all through life— 'learn to be.'"[4]

Capacity to Formulate Mission

What people will do throughout their lives will undoubtedly change with respect to occupational pursuits, modes of communication and transportation, energy sources, food, leisure time activities, and family patterns. Therefore, just as the individual needs education to be himself, to "become himself," whatever the circumstances, so do institutions with this aim require similar characteristics themselves. What they will do cannot now be precisely stated. What is needed is institutional capability to determine what is appropriate and needed in given circumstances. And for this capability, we must look to qualities of institutional "being."

In our search for mission these qualities have already been postulated. They emerged out of a melange of discussion, observation, and reflection. They do not describe what the institution is to do. They are not a mission statement, but they could well be considered as requisite elements in a community college capable of formulating its mission. They occur with pronounced frequency in community colleges usually judged to be superior.

1. The college is adaptable. It is capable of change in response to new conditions and demands, or circumstances.
2. The college operates with a continuing awareness of its community.
3. The college has continuing relationships with the learner.
4. The college extends opportunity to the "unserved."
5. The college accommodates to diversity.
6. The college has a nexus function in the community's learning system.

One could question the words used. For example, does adaptable mean that the institution is always influenced by its community and does not play a role in shaping that community? More appropriately, adaptability also carries the connotation that the organization has a relationship that improves its capabilities to function in its environment. It will help shape as well as be shaped. Is "awareness" a strong enough term? Without going into extended detail, "awareness" would seem to be a very strong concept. The organization is alive, alert, utilizing its senses to probe for meaning in environmental signals and cues. Awareness suggests broad rather than tunnel vision. It implies a positive, anticipatory stance.

Some may question diversity as an essential element. The view here is of diversity as a contributing factor in the learning process for those who are "learning to be."

Concerns about institutional mission are understandable. Change is often unsettling. Perceived competitors vie for territory we have occupied. New voices tell us what to do. We are held accountable for developments that appear to be outside our control. And the conventional methods of projecting future developments are not working.

We and those who appropriate funds for the institutions would undoubtedly find it a decided relief, we imagine, to have a clean, precise, and specific description of what the institutions are to do. But that cannot be done on a national level. Perhaps not even at the state level. And in the individual institution it must be a continuing process, not once and for all. What can be sought at national and state levels is for the establishment of conditions that allow institutions to be capable of determining suitable actions within broad policy guidelines. Of greatest concern to those interested in appropriate learning opportunities should be the continuing viability of the organization rather than a catalogue of its services.

Repeatedly, we have referred to the tendency to respond to questions of mission in terms of institutional programs. We have said that the fact of rapid change in our society and the dissimilarity of communities repudiate the utility of such an approach. However, a general statement would be of value and it is not entirely beyond our reach. It is therefore proposed as a synthesis of considerations presented in this chapter that the mission of community colleges be stated in this fashion: *To encourage and facilitate lifelong learning, with community as process and product.*

---

[1] R. H. Dave. *Foundations of Lifelong Education.* Paris: UNESCO, 1976, p. 15.

[2] Edgar Faure et al. *Learning to Be: The World of Education Today and Tomorrow.* Paris: UNESCO, 1972, p. 13.

[3] Ibid. p. 196.

[4] Ibid. p. vi.

Chapter II

FOCUS ON EDUCATION FOR COMMUNITY DEVELOPMENT

Americans going to other countries to live for a time, representing corporations or government, most likely would be prepared for their assignments through programs that require not only learning appropriate languages but many other aspects of the host culture. The results of sending people without training have proved disastrous.

All Americans will have the experience (limited, of course, by the terms of their existence) of living in a different culture—that of the future. Preparation for that excursion is complicated by lack of knowledge of what that culture will be like. And whatever it is, it will not stay the same. It will continue to change. That being the case, there can be no stopping point in learning (except cessation of existence). And what is to be learned will be much broader in scope than the curricula of former years which, by and large, prepared people to ''go out into the world'' and take up occupations or pursue careers.

In addition to the learning requirements imposed by changing culture and environment, changes in the maturation of the individual will affect educational needs. Several contemporary writers describe the "passages" or developmental stages in the lives of individuals and the tasks that require learning for successful transit through those periods. All of this is to say that the notion of who needs education, when it is needed, and for what, is itself in process of change.

Who Needs Education?

Answers to those questions may be affected partially by an element in our culture that will likely be extended into the culture of the future. Our society, notwithstanding obvious omissions, has a broadening sense of responsibility for those in need. Motivations that produced social legislation may be mixed; nevertheless, our society has made provision for support of large numbers of people who are unemployed, sick, poor, living in inadequate housing, and retired from worthwhile occupations.

Aggravated by inflation, financial costs to support a dependent population continue to mount. A typical illustration is found in the general fund budget of the State of Michigan where social services as a percentage of the general fund budget in 1962-63 was 16.5%. In the governor's recommendation for 1979-80, it was 29.8%, the largest item in the budget.

If it were not for welfare programs and social aid, the International Labor Organization reports, one of every four American families would live below the official poverty line. The major cause of poverty, the study said, is that the poor cannot find appropriate employment because they are either unsuitably trained or lack the necessary skills.

Grave concerns have been expressed by economists about the adequacy of retirement programs to support the mounting proportion of older people in the United States in relation to the number of employed who are contributing to Social Security. Less than two years after Congress thought it had put Social Security in order for the rest of this century, the Congressional Budget Office warned that inflation and recession are again buffeting the old age trust fund and that a legislative remedy is required. A proposal has been made to pay for the Medicare program of Social Security from general tax revenues.

In what certainly must be a related matter, Joseph Califano, the former secretary of Health, Education, and Welfare, in a foreword to the Surgeon General's Report in late 1979, called for a second public health revolution in the country. In response to the Report's announcement that deaths from such "degenerative diseases" as heart ailments, stroke, and cancer have increased sharply, accounting for 75 percent of all deaths in the U.S., he urged that the "nation's health strategy be dramatically recast" to emphasize the prevention of disease through changes in life style and personal conduct, as well as through medical advances. Among the points made in the report are the following:

Cigarette smoking is the single most preventable cause of death. Alcohol is a factor in more than 10 percent of all deaths in the U.S. Americans are eating too much sugar, salt, red meat, fat and cholesterol and not enough whole grains, cereals, fruits, vegetables, fish, poultry and legumes.

Up to 20 percent of all cancer deaths may be linked to exposure to chemicals and other hazards on the job.

Injuries account for half of all the deaths of persons between the ages of 15 and 24.

Learning to Produce

If we are concerned about the rising costs to support large numbers of dependent people, does it not make sense to consider what can be done to help them become productive, contributing citizens? The International Labor Organization asserts that the poor cannot find appropriate employment because "they are either unsuitably trained or lack the necessary skills." Degenerative diseases which appear to be related to life style and personal conduct increase in incidence with consequent increases in medical costs. Life styles and personal conduct are a product of learning. In the near future, if trends continue, one working person will be supporting two who are retired. Would it not be in the self-interest of the nation and our communities for citizens to be self-reliant, self-supporting, and able to contribute for as long as possible?

The argument so far for suitable education and training for employment, disease prevention, and what might be called "positive aging," has been to ease the load of the taxpayer by proportionately reducing the numbers who are limited in paying their own way. Although not possessing as much political appeal at this time, the strongest case for learning how to secure certain basic necessities such as health, employment, and housing surely is in what happens to the individual in terms of self-confidence, pride, and a sense of usefulness.

In the face of what would seem to be evident good sense, it is puzzling that education is seldom viewed by policymakers at federal and state levels as a dynamic resource in community development and in addressing significant and expensive problems that confront our society.

Possibly the answer lies both in somewhat limited perceptions of policy makers and the variable attitudes of educators. It would seem that it is time to affirm that *a primary function of community colleges is to aid those in the community who want to learn how to secure certain basic necessities. Among these are: housing, health, employment, food, and citizenship rights and responsibilities.*

Learning to Cope

Moreover, there are other developments in the environment that require people to learn skills for coping. For example, changes in energy sources and costs will substantially affect our way of life. Not only are new technologies and technologists required, but at the individual, family, and community levels, information is required, judgments of value must be made, and patterns of behavior established to deal with the high cost of energy as a new fact in our lives.

Related to a mood of frustration at energy and inflation problems and possibly with its roots in the social ferment of the sixties, is a call for simplification in organizational life and increased self-reliance of individuals and families. Sometimes called appropriate technology (AT), a new movement is gathering followers who aim toward the best use of scarce resources, usually on a small scale. Appropriate technology includes solar heated homes, wood stoves, windmills, basement fish tanks, recycled garbage, and organically grown food. It is also community health programs that stress preventive care rather than expensive surgery. It is financing for small businesses and credit unions. It is a school that teaches children how to teach themselves. It is blacksmiths. And weavers. And do-it-yourself carpentry.

The appropriate technology movement has led to home weatherization, community development corporations, sweat-equity housing, inner-city food co-ops, solar greenhouses, all aimed at increasing self-reliance for those with fixed, modest, or low incomes. There is also support among people who favor local control, community economic development, and/or community self-reliance. AT in the eyes of some observers may hold promise for stabilizing local economies, reducing living costs, allowing wiser use of local resources, and/or regaining control of basic needs and life-support systems.

Does the community college have a role to play in the development of appropriate technologies? It has been said that the community college, with its emphasis on community development, establishing linkages, and launching cooperative ventures with other community institutions, not only has a role to play but that it *is* an appropriate technology.

Providing the Educational Component

A community college in Illinois provides a case in point. It demonstrated its capabilities in this regard through the part it played in dealing with a serious housing problem in the city of Aurora, Illinois. It should be noted that the board of trustees of the college adopted a policy statement some years ago which gave reason to subsequent activities:

> It shall be the policy of the Board to provide a comprehensive community services program. Community services are defined as those efforts of the community college, usually undertaken in cooperation with other community groups or agencies, which are directed toward identifying and analyzing community social, economic, cultural and civic problems and providing the educational component of their solution.

Waubonsee Community College does not offer a "laundry list" of courses with the assumption that students will register in those which they consider relevant to their needs. Rather, it has developed a strategic and tactical approach with these steps:

1. Maintain continuous and intimate involvement in the service area, so that the institution is immediately aware of community needs.
2. Focus on community issues as they emerge and develop cosponsored task forces or ad hoc committees in cooperation with other interested community institutions, groups, and individuals. The task force, or community advisory committee, is tailored to the particular issue.
3. Initiate workshops, seminars, and conferences (e.g., community forums) to study the issue and to develop solutions.
4. The College then designs and executes educational programs which satisfy the needs of the solution from an educational per-

spective. Other agencies, newly formed if necessary, provide the needed non-educational components.

Edward Fauth, dean of community services, reports that in July, 1975, there was acute community concern in Aurora (population 80,000) about housing. Sensing this, college officials initiated an exploratory planning meeting. With the invitations went these questions:

1. How do we build housing that people can afford with a reasonable portion of their family income?
2. How can we enforce reasonable building codes, and still have a place into which displaced families can move?
3. How can we prevent further deterioration of neighborhoods and rehabilitate already sub-standard housing, with available resources?
4. How can low-income housing be dispersed equitably among neighboring communities?
5. What is the answer to the "red-lining" question and the responsibility of financial institutions to the people who invest their savings in them?

Interest was high. Attendance was good. A sub-committee was established and an ad hoc housing committee was organized. Contacts were established with the Federal Home Loan Bank and the U.S. Department of Housing and Urban Development. The program developed involved a high degree of local initiative and control, and appealed to the conservative nature of the community. An agreement was entered into with the FHLB-HUD for a one-year feasibility study which confirmed the existence of community need, interest, and resources. Consequently, a not-for-profit corporation, Neighborhod Housing Services of Aurora, Inc., was formed and tax exemption obtained. Membership of the board of directors included persons from local government, lending institutions, community representatives, a realtor, and one staff member from the community college. NHS results to date include:

1. The inspection and rehabilitation to code of homes in several model blocks.
2. A demonstrable increase in conventional loans in the target area.
3. Low interest rate loans to qualified homeowners, such as senior citizens.
4. Establishment of a growing number of block organizations in the area.

5. Improved, although not yet ideal, communication and understanding among the NHS partners of neighborhood residents, local government, and lending institutions. WCC staff have been able to contribute to this accomplishment, through the conduct of board workshops and nominal group sessions at critical times.
6. A community education program described by the executive director of NHS as"necessary for the success of the loan and rehabilitation services offered by his organization. As the area changes to more owner-occupied homes, we're going to need this kind of education to assist home owners."

Four courses were determined to be useful by NHS and WCC.

1. Basic Home Maintenance Series
2. Basic Kitchen Remodeling/Direct Experience
3. Basic Home and Consumer Finance
4. Energy Conservation in the Home

Dr. Fauth describes the Neighborhood Housing Services of Aurora, Inc., as a development which illustrates the role that a community college can play in working toward the solution of a high priority state and local problem. In his estimation, it covers the complete spectrum of problem solving from needs assessment, through analyzing the problem and developing alternative solutions, and furnishing the educational component of the solution.

Other high priority community problems have been approached from the same policy base and by using similar strategies and tactics. A study was conducted in the district in 1977 with results supporting the hypothesis that public service activity of the type conducted by the college over a period of years generates significant citizen/ taxpayer support for the college and for the program. The conclusions of that study may have been confirmed in December, 1978, by an educational tax rate referendum. The referendum was successful by a five-to-one ratio in a climate pervaded by the property tax cutting Proposition 13 initiative in California.

Rising Social Costs

Housing needs are easy to observe. Anybody can see buildings that are deteriorating, that apartments or houses are not available, or that no new construction is under way. On the other hand, there is a development in our society, of which we have only lately become aware, that has extraordinary significance in terms of financial and human costs (and benefits, too) for our communities: older people.

When asked about educational needs and how their institutions would respond during the next ten years, community college personnel were in total agreement that a fundamental change is taking place with regard to the place of older people in this country. The colleges expect to give much more attention to the upper end of the age spectrum as men and women in that category look for ways to prepare for new careers, learn more about handling their finances, or prepare for the psychological and biological adjustments of old age.

A growing flow of evidence graphically reveals the inadequacy and even the cruelty of present social arrangements for people at and beyond the conventional age of retirement. The problems (and the possibilities—after all, the lifespan is extending) are not confined to the United States. Jan Helander, director of the Gerontological Center at Lund, Sweden, comments:

> "To enjoy one's otium" is a common expression for turning pensioner. The Latin word "otium" means "idleness." It would seem that, regardless of reason, one stops enjoying it fairly quickly. One question is whether society has perhaps created a welfare device that does not merely create welfare. A second question would then be to what extent this device is such an artificial interference in our life rhythm that the consequence is an increased need for care. A third question is how much society has to pay for this increased need for care and if that is the best way to spend that money.

The critical nature of the problem is emphasized by Dr. Helander in a reference to a meeting of the Council of Europe in November 1975 concerning "the changing population structures in Europe and rising social costs." The main topic was the future care of older persons. Quoting from the discussions:

> We are faced with a future which includes an explosion of the costs for the care of older people. This implies that there will be a lack of funds in a number of countries. Already today we have to understand that in these countries it will be impossible to take care of old people in the way we happen to be used to. Alternatives have to be found.

Something to Live For

While the Council of Europe report highlights financial costs, another voice describes a cost which may be even more troubling. In Japan there are nine million people over age 65 and their numbers are steadily increasing. One of Japan's leading industrialists, Konosuke Matsushita, founder of the world-wide electric and home appliance organization, Matsushita Electric, was asked what he thought ought to be done in response to the general trend in Japan and around the world for the growing numbers of older people. In a recent issue of *PHP*, a magazine published in Japan, he said:

> Of all the many things that have been suggested, I think emphasis should be laid on giving old people an appropriate *ikigai*—a goal, something to live for, a purpose in life. This would eliminate loneliness, the feeling of being unwanted and gradually cut off from the society, which I believe is one of the most painful and fundamental of problems in old age. Most concern for old people is concentrated more on figuring out what kind of facilities or welfare system to provide for them. Hardly any importance is placed on meeting their psychological needs, when actually the most important thing for them is to have something worth living for. There are many kinds of ikigai that would work, but I would say the most effective one would be for them to have a job to do and place to do it in, in society.

Lars Ulvenstam, cultural counsellor of the Swedish Embassy in Washington, reports many in-depth interviews with elderly persons in Sweden showed the longer people live in good health and the more the working environment can be improved, the more citizens will want to continue daily lives without drastic changes.

> We will not be satisfied with therapy in a center for retired people or an old age home, where we sit and sandpaper semi-manufactured goods into wooden spoons, candlesticks or footstools . . . Give me anything in which I can make a contribution. IF SOCIETY DOES NOT listen, there is a risk that many older people will become bitter and unhappy . . .

Soon, it is reported, in the State of Florida 30 percent of the population will be older than 60-65. And a statewide organization known as the Silver-Haired Legislature has organized to inform the elected state officials of interests and needs of older persons that may be affected by legislative means. Educational opportunity ranks high among priorities.

One of the world's largest communities of retired people (some 20,000) is located in Southern California in an area served by Saddleback Community College. Described as intelligent and in good health, the great majority of the residents are from professional and executive areas of experience. They want to do things. Four thousand of them are enrolled in community college courses. Interests include health, nutrition, exercise, and a wide range of other subjects.

Manhattan Community College in New York City has an arrangement with the Institute for the Study of Older Adults, based at New York City Community College, for the administration of centers in Manhattan to serve older people. Sixteen centers are now functioning with 12-20 people whose age range is 55 to more than 70. The participants are retired and have educational backgrounds of perhaps four to eight years. The needs vary. There is usually a course in basic English. Requests have been made by older people for what amounts to an additional 84 centers which, in effect, are on a waiting list.

The program is supported by an annual grant from the Agency for Aging. College leaders say that a program of this kind is central to their mission, as they see it, but on the other hand, the Board of Higher Education and the budget say it is not. Views of the faculty are mixed. Some say, "We are part of the City University of New York and need to behave that way." Others say, "We ought to meet the needs of the unserved." In commenting in particular about an area of Broadway above 42nd Street, the president of the college mused:

> There are many lonely old people sitting on the benches gasping in the carbon monoxide. They have no family. They are not served by anyone. There ought to be 50 or more centers for them. These lonely people living in a hotel room desperately need services such as could be provided by this institution.

What of these lonely old people "not served by anyone?" Is society, in fact, creating a welfare device that creates welfare? Can anything be done about the explosion of costs for care of older people? Authorities assert that alternatives must be found. What are they? What conditions are required for older people to have a goal, something to do, something to live for? What is society's response to the assertions by many of the retired that they "want to do things?" How do we deal with the possibility of a serious schism between young and old as the old become "bitter and unhappy," and the young resentful at carrying the mounting load of financial support for all of society?

In the face of social and learning needs of such great proportions, it is unthinkable that a community educational institution could say "this is not our business." And the colleges are stepping up their activities. But the pace of response still lags far behind the demands of emerging reality.

Aging Begins Early

Comprehensive descriptions of what community colleges are doing are given in other publications. My purpose here is to deal with the basic rationale. It is most important to acknowledge that the process of aging does not start at the time of retirement. The aging process begins at conception. We are told the frontal lobe of the brain, which creates and thinks, does not age until we are really old. And that aging of the brain should be prevented by using the frontal lobe as much as possible.

Apparently the quality of the "last of life" is directly related to the quality of earlier years. If learning is cultivated throughout a lifetime, the attitudes, skills, and understandings through which one moves into the later developmental stages are shaped in a continuing process. Although programs directly addressed to older people are of value, the most significant contribution of the community college over the long run is to encourage and facilitate learning with community as process and product.

Improving Government

What are the other community problems that press for attention? "Government citizen relationships" headed the list in a University of Illinois study of what people are concerned about. The so-called tax revolt of the late 1970's has been attributed in part to dissatisfaction by the public with how its business is conducted and what the taxpayers are getting for their money. A number of community colleges collaborate with other community organizations in educational programs that aim at improving the proficiency of government employees.

Within two years after the San Francisco Community College District was formed in 1970, its leaders met with representatives of city, county, state, and federal agencies. A series of workshops considered the training needs and the development of educational services required for pre-entry, refresher, in-service, and promotional programs for the more than 40,000 public service employees in San Francisco. The result was co-sponsorship of the Civil Service

College, operated by the community college district with five major curriculum areas:

1. Supervision and Management: pre-supervision, first-line supervision, middle and top management
2. Clerical and Secretarial: all office skills and performance tests
3. Communication: language and speech arts and foreign languages
4. Community Services: e.g., city-wide training under affirmative action guidelines in preparation for the position of Firefighter and of Police Officer
5. Technical, as requested: e.g., principles and practices of occupational safety and health

A faculty of 75 instructors in this public service college conduct some 350 classes of 80 course offerings at 33 locations—in practically every public building in the city. All Civil Service College classes are offered tuition free. However, in return for this free instructional service, the participating government agencies provide free training and conference rooms. And the co-sponsoring government agencies contribute instructional aids and materials that may be required.

An unanticipated result has been a cross-fertilization not only across departmental lines but across levels of government, ranging from local to federal. Training and personnel officers among the various agencies are in touch with each other. Well over 10 percent of the 40,000 city, county, state, and federal employees are enrolled in a given year, with the median student at 36-41 years of age, head of a family, experienced in college-level study, veteran of more than five years of government service, preparing for promotional opportunities as well as for increased competence in current job activities.

To Build Better Citizen Boards

There is another facet of community organization to which community colleges are giving attention. Much of community business in the United States is conducted by citizen boards. Board members find their responsibilities mounting for many reasons, sometimes to the point of discouraging qualified personnel from service. Public demands for accountability, the complexities of collective bargaining agreements with employees, and an increasing tendency for recourse to litigation in matters of dispute are among factors commonly encountered. The pressures put on a board, particularly in times of financial stress, to assure good management of an enterprise are also significant factors.

Spearheaded by Kellogg Community College and supported by the W. K. Kellogg Foundation, Michigan community colleges are engaged in a program designed to build better citizen boards. Specifically, the goal is to encourage the involvement of Michigan community colleges in assisting voluntary board members in (1) understanding their duties and responsibilities, (2) creating better relationships among agencies, (3) improving relationships among board members, (4) utilizing the skills and talents of board members, and (5) attracting effective board members from the community. Every community will have from hundreds to thousands of people serving on boards of colleges, libraries, hospitals, youth organizations, service clubs, the United Way, and many other institutions. The implications for community life are surely self-evident. The health and proficiency of the voluntary sector of our society is at least as important as the governmental; in fact, one could say that the vitality of one is directly related to the vitality of the other.

Community Research

A basic element in community development is community research—identification of problems, needs, and possibilities in the service area of the college. It has been orthodox litany that the community college does not engage in research. That profession has been enunciated for too long. Community colleges cannot exercise their "awareness" function without scientific investigation or inquiry—that is, "research." The focus of research will be influenced by elements of community college function that have already been presented. For example, research will be oriented to practical problems. Results will be applied to a community problem or need, very likely as a college program or one in which several community agencies collaborate.

An example of that kind of research is found at the Fashion Institute of Technology in New York. Although the institution involved is specialized, the kind of assistance it provides its community, the fashion industry, can be extrapolated to the experience of more comprehensive institutions.

FIT received a $100,000 grant from the state legislature, alarmed at the out-migration of the apparel industry from the city of New York and from the state, to support a research effort as to the causes. There were those who assumed that cheaper wage rates in the South were responsible, but other signals from the industry indicated that this was only partially true. There had been no effective search to ascertain the real issues. With better understanding of the problem, the loss of industry, it was hoped, could be thwarted.

It was found that the lure of low wage rates elsewhere was not the real cause. Rather, in New York City and in the state the manufacturers were technologically deficient. Plant layouts were poor. Knowledge of modern machinery was lacking, and the manufacturers were not competitive with their counterparts in other parts of the country. The industry was being enticed by other states with promises of better conditions for doing business.

Technical Assistance

As a result of the study and subsequent action by the state legislature, the New York sewn products industry is receiving technical assistance through a program developed by the Fashion Institute of Technology. A $250,000 grant was made to the college for a four-pronged approach. A publication, *Spin*, the sewn products newsletter, presents to New York manufacturers and contractors in summary form new developments in technology and equipment, government regulations, basic production information and tips on manufacturing techniques, as well as notices of seminars and trade shows. FIT established a hands-on display and testing center at the college for the use of manufacturers and contractors in determining equipment needs.

Technical and production-oriented seminars are being held in New York City and at appropriate sites for manufacturers located up-state. Seminars cover a wide range of topics and provide training in repair and maintenance of modern production machinery.

In addition, a program has been developed to furnish external engineering consulting services for small to medium-sized manufacturers and contractors. Engineers with backgrounds in production technology provide specialized knowledge to personnel who would otherwise lack the means to acquire these services. The program is expected to result in the improvement of industrial technology in the state and in the forging of new links between the state government and manufacturers and contractors in New York, and consequently retaining jobs in New York and encouraging growth possibilities.

Technology Transfer

A somewhat different model for provision of technical assistance has been developed by 10 community colleges in southeastern Michigan. The program is called SEMTAP—Southeastern Michigan Technical Assistance Program—and is operated in conjunction with the Environmental Research Institute in Ann Arbor (ERIM). ERIM, a free-standing institute, participates by conducting research which is responsive to local needs and in making results available to local communities through the community colleges. In the field of energy utilization, for example, ERIM has come up with findings that have practical application through college programs for house builders, insulation contractors, and home owners in providing effective and economical measures to conserve energy through minimizing heat loss.[1]

There is considerable evidence that community colleges in partnership with organizations active in research and development can deliver services and elicit participation of local organizations on a wide range of domestic problems—health, transportation, energy, environment, housing, economic development, agriculture, and aging. The approach is similar to that of the agricultural extension services broadened to other fields and using the vast network of community-based institutions.

An impressive research and development operation exists in this country which a few years ago was centered on space and defense. Now many domestic problems are under study in areas such as those cited above. What is needed is a structure that integrates this massive research and development community with problems and people at the local level. SEMTAP has established a pilot program that deserves replication in many other parts of the country as change requires new knowledge and its application to community development.

Community Assimilation

Previously in this chapter it was said that a primary function of the community college is to aid those in the community who want to learn how to secure certain basic necessities. One of those necessities cited was "citizenship rights and responsibilities." The fact that the most frequently taught "foreign" language in community colleges is English as a Second Language provides a clue to the characteristics of many of the people served by these institutions. They seek a functioning place in a society not native to them. Often the changes they encounter can be traumatic in effect. Developments in Southeast Asia during the last several years have forced large number of immigrants to seek new homes, jobs, and a sense of acceptance and usefulness in a country far different from their own. They are not the most numerous of the immigrants. They are not the first, nor will they be the last, but they illustrate an essential contribution which the community college can make toward facilitating a sense of "community."

Evelyn Haught, a lecturer in English at Northern Virginia Community College, reported her impressions in the *Washington Post*. She commented on the increasing prominence of Vietnamese "in arenas in which we customarily find immigrant influence only after two or three generations: in the teaching profession, in medicine, in the church and in non-ethnic business enterprise."

Haught asks what accounts for this rapid assimilation. Why have they risen so quickly? She concedes that sociologists might have many explanations, but she suggests that the Vietnamese have had access to one social and economic ladder that earlier immigrants did not have: the community college system.

According to Ms. Haught, Northern Virginia Community College has itself helped literally thousands of Vietnamese in the last six years and she describes some of these people:

S_____ Nfuyen, in 1973, was trying desperately to maintain some sort of grasp on a rapidly disintegrating life; in 1977, he was an engineering student at the college, possessed of enough confidence to argue, and win, a classroom debate on the merits of Faulkner over Hemingway.

H_____ Dinh, at age 60, once a bureaucrat in Saigon, is now an A student writing English themes along with other freshmen. His dream: to use his fiscal abilities in the U.S. government.

T_____ Tran was formerly a well-known novelist in Vietnam. When he arrived in the United States, he worked as a janitor so he could earn his tuition. In a short time, he left behind his mops and brooms and became a coordinator of Vietnamese student concerns in the Fairfax County public school system. At the college, he is studying art with a goal of becoming a commercial artist.

The writer cites her own family experiences as a basis for the high value she places on the community college role in assimilation.

> My own immigrant father fled Mussolini's Italy to build a new life and succeeded beyond even his own expectations. Yet he never felt as though he had become one of us, a real American. Until the end of his life he remained embarrassed by his lack of an American education. In 1939, there was nothing comparable to the community college system, and a poor, frightened Italian boy who spoke little English couldn't even hope to enter the state university.

> That is the role the community college now plays for the Vietnamese. It gives them an opportunity to mix quickly with other Americans of every intellectual and social level, of every race, and to know in doing so that they are really welcome and well-regarded.

Education as a Resource

The kind of education we are considering directly addresses critical needs in our society. It deals with real "basics"—housing, aging, employment, quality of community life, citizenship, and how to deal with the emerging future. It fulfills the mandate stated so forcefully by the late Peter Goldmark—inventor and humanitarian:

> There is no longer time to educate the next generation; the solutions must be found now. Hence, learning of on-going issues and problems such as crime, energy, conservation, health care, etc., and the newly required planning processes to deal with them, present a newly evolving and urgent task for the nation's educational institutions, one which they have never faced before.

But travel this country and talk to people in high position about the future of education and they speak generally of decline. Their emphasis is upon shrinking enrollments in the eighties and nineties, changes in clientele and shifts among disciplines, but there is little reference to how educational resources can be utilized to address substantial social and economic problems that perplex us. For example, in a working paper prepared by a task force on the future of Illinois, a section deals with education.

> Higher education is an extremely valuable resource in Illinois. The institutions of higher education provide special training for particular occupations and a broad background for many occupations. These institutions are facing a number of problems. The major ones are declining enrollments, changing student clientele and demands for

programs and, most important, defining its evolving role in the state.

It is precisely that definition of evolving role that is not forthcoming. In another state a budget official was asked whether the economic report of the governor which projected economic problems and objectives included any reference to the contribution of educational institutions. The response was negative but it was conceded that the question was a fair one.

To Deal with Community Problems

Limited perceptions of the role education can play in meeting needs of people are reflected in what the state and community will pay for in terms of educational services. Currently a good deal of attention is directed toward an attempt to distinguish between what some perceive to be of obvious academic merit and that which seems peripheral. Although more attention will be given to this issue in the chapter on funding, it should be noted here that courses given for academic credit which apply toward university transfer or direct preparation for an occupation are considered legitimate candidates for public support. However, many services related to the areas of need described in this chapter do not now qualify in the same manner. Attempts are under way in several states to carefully describe educational activities that contribute toward community development and which are beyond the conventional credit and degree pathways. For example, in order to qualify for support from the community instructional services fund in the State of Florida, an educational activity must meet each of the following criteria:

A. The courses need planned, non-credit instructional activity which is based on a significant community problem.

1. Each course must be justified on the basis of the expected contribution it will make to the identification and solution of community problems, hence, the first concern in programming these courses is the identification of problems which in the judgment of the coordinating council for vocational education, adult general education, and community instructional services have significance to the community and should be categorized under the following definitions:

a. environmental problems which relate to the development, use and conservation of natural resources.

b. problems relating to health and safety which are based on provisions for the development and maintenance of physical and emotional health of the people as well as for the protection of the people against natural and man-made hazards.

c. human relations problems which relate to the interaction of groups of people in the community and to the need for the development or maintenance of a common set of values and aspirations.

d. governmental problems which relate to the organization and operation of agencies needed to maintain services to the people.

e. problems relating to education and child rearing which are based on provisions in the community for rearing children and for the education of children, youth, and adults.

f. consumer economics problems which relate to the production, distribution and consumption of goods and services.

2. As a planned educational activity, each course is to have clearly defined expected outcomes which relate to a significant problem in one or more of the above categories. The outcomes which justify a course fall within the following two categories (1) there will be an increased understanding of the specific community problem and of alternatives for the solution of the problem, and (2) citizens will acquire knowledge and skills which they need in order to cope with and to help solve these problems.[2]

The Florida statement is useful in several ways. There is recognition that "non-credit" instructional activity can be of value and worthy of state financial support. The importance is attached to education that deals with environmental factors affecting the lives of people in the community setting: natural resources, health and safety, social interaction, governmental operations, consumer economics, and family organization. The necessity for planning toward specified outcomes is emphasized, properly so. Not the least of the benefits will be to allay anxieties of those who are responsible for financial appropriations about using tax funds for education which moves beyond traditional preparation of youth.

A question must be raised, however, about how to take a further step. Repeated use is made of the word "course." Are there not learning activities required for community development that may more effectively use other modes to accomplish their purposes? Course has a bit of the flavor of "horseless carriage" and "wireless."

Public Service

Community colleges in the State University of New York refer to the community development dimension of their work as "public service." Thus, they benefit from inclusion in the university network with its stipulated threefold program of teaching, research, and public service. The 1976 master plan of the State University of New York (including the community colleges) contains the following commitment:

> In addition to the pursuit and augmentation of those campus efforts which normally serve the respective communities, the University as a whole will mount a statewide effort to identify the major public problems at all levels and the University capabilities which could best contribute to the solution of such problems and bring about a still more direct mobilization of effort in terms of public service. The redevelopment of the economy and the maintenance of efficient and effective social services, for example, will be matters of major concern to the University.

> . . . among the three missions of universities, teaching, research and public service, the State University pursues the mission of public service concretely and seriously just as it pursues the other two. In the great majority of activities public service is not a specially or separately funded effort depending upon expenditure of additional state tax dollars. Rather it tends to be carved out either through special application of capabilities already in existence or through funding on a project basis by non-state clients or sources.

Mohawk Valley Community College sponsors an industry-labor, education council. Jamestown Community College sends faculty, referred to as "brokers," into the community to identify problems and to determine the kinds of services the college can provide to solve the problems. Cayuga County Community College recently drew more than 1,000 senior citizens for a one day free program featuring health tests and seminars on financial matters and other concerns. Monroe Community College offers "client specific" programs to business and industry. These are credit-free, tailor-made courses or programs provided at the request and for the benefit of local business or non-profit organizations. An employment and training catalogue is widely distributed. More than a dozen programs are currently conducted on site, that is, on the employer's premises.

The Cooperative Mode

Call it community instructional services, or public service, or community development, one must be impressed by the variety and ingenuity of ways in which community colleges relate to social and economic needs and problems in their areas. The degree of involvement varies, apparently, with different views of appropriateness and with respect to what the college is authorized to do under law and regulations. (Incidently, the determination of what is feasible and legal appears to differ among institutions within the same legal framework.) Viewing the panorama of institutional activities in this field suggests three general types of behavior:

Reaction. The college responds to an obvious need, or pressure, or request and goes into action upon determination of profitability or economic feasibility.

Direction. The college uses a more sophisticated and somewhat more inner-directed approach, analyzes the community to identify problems and then makes recommendations or proposals.

Cooperation. The college, through analysis or cooperative exploration with the community, identifies a problem and initiates a process or provides resources to help the *community* solve it. Although the solution might involve community college courses or programs and personnel, the impetus comes from the community with college encouragement and counsel. The college in effect contributes "process." The community, being mover and partner, benefits in greater degree because of its own involvement.

Not many examples of this kind of approach come to mind. Relatively few colleges have had the capability in staff to undertake cooperative efforts of this kind or have envisioned such action as appropriate. But that picture is changing. Waubonsee Community College, as cited earlier, played this role in its initiatives with regard to housing. Other institutions, some of them referred to in this chapter, are moving in the same direction and with good reason, for it is in the cooperative relationship that the greatest benefits are promised to community and college.

The community benefits from a college that is:

A research arm to identify problems objectively and to project probable developments;

A forum for nonpartisan informed discussion of issues and proposed policies;

An organization to facilitate learning; and

A nexus for relating the teaching/learning resources of the community.

And what of the benefits to the college? It is through the *cooperative* mode that the community college achieves its distinctiveness. It is to serve the community and it is to do more than that. It is to be creatively occupied with the community. It is the community's college, a vital part of an integrated system of community services. If it limits itself to the conventional academic area, no matter how great its numbers might become or how excellent its programs, it remains the lower level of a pyramid of academic prestige with the graduate school as the cap.

Toward Community

But in the community setting the college is on familiar terrain. It functions in a complex of organizations designed to provide for people's basic needs and to enliven and enrich their lives. And in working with organizations, agencies, bureaus, the policy-setting groups, and the decision makers, the college finds the surest ground for communication—shared effort and common participation.

The word "common," or in the Latin, *communis*, is the root word for both "community" and "communication." When we speak of community, we mean more than people living in the same locality, even more than people with a common interest. We envision a condition where people learn to communicate, where there can be a sense of connection and interchange of thoughts and ideas. To *develop* "community" means to expand or realize the potentialities of the place and the people and "to bring gradually to a fuller, greater, or better state." The community college that focuses on education for community development participates in that process.

[1] According to recent reports, American houses ''leak oil from almost every pore.'' Proper measures could cut heating costs in half ''without touching a single thermostat.'' *New York Times*, July 22, 1979.

[2] Florida State Board of Education. *Administrative Rules for the Operation of Florida's Community/Junior Colleges.* Supplement No. 88. Tallahassee: the Board, 1978.

Chapter III

RELATING TO OTHER COMMUNITY AGENCIES

The story is told of the weary mother of 10 who demurred when her husband suggested that another child would be desirable. He replied by reference to the Scriptures, "Be fruitful, multiply, and replenish the earth." Her response was a gentle, "But we don't have to do it all."

Community colleges encourage and facilitate learning in the community. But they do not do it all. Continuous learning is a concept to be implanted as a goal of the *individual*. It is not the domain of any single institution. Within the broad reach of its mission, the college will establish goals that take into account its own capacities and resources as well as those of other organizations in its area.

As has been observed earlier, the community college has the potential for serving a connecting and linking function among parts of the community learning system. The entire complex will provide educational services and resources far beyond those possible from any one of the institutions that make it up.

Values in Cooperation

Insistent calls are heard now for more cooperation and coordination among providers of educational services, especially those that receive public funds so that possible duplication and overlap can be minimized. State officials, editorial writers, and educators are expressing concerns that everybody is getting on the adult learning bandwagon, perhaps motivated more by institutional self-interest than by improving the well-being of the new clientele.

Coordination with the intent of consolidating resources and possibly trimming costs does make sense. Coordination is also essential for another good reason sometimes overlooked in today's cost-sensitive atmosphere. Large numbers of our society are not participating in adult learning activities. As we observe many institutions with eyes on the adult education "market," we may note that, in general, those institutions are going after the same people. Even as research shows that the number of participants in education is growing, the number of those *not* participating is increasing at a greater rate. Those *not* participating are of lower income levels, of older years, of limited education, and many of them are not white.[1]

A recent study of illiteracy in the United States reported that efforts to eradicate illiteracy among adults were "grossly inadequate," and that "new and varied approaches are needed to help tens of millions of adults who lack the skills to perform basic tasks."

> Only by intensive attention will they be reached by an educational program. Many will never enroll in programs of any sort for diverse reasons: cultural or linguistic barriers, fear of failing, distrust of the institutions of the mainstream culture, reliance on electronic media as a substitute for the written word, and the ability of some to find satisfaction despite low levels of academic attainment.[2]

An informal, community-based approach to literacy education is proposed by the authors to win the confidence of people who would otherwise be suspicious of solutions that they consider imposed upon them from the outside.

A cooperative approach of community organizations should result in a diversified array of services and resources to accommodate to marked differences among the population in styles of learning, financial resources, motivations, interests, time available, and convenience of location.

To achieve economies *and* to assure that educational services are available to all sectors of the population, particularly to those whose options appear to be limited, there is need to coordinate. The cooperative stance will also assure the availability of greater resources. For example, the manager of a large plant of a heavy equipment manufacturer points out the need for people to be trained on up-to-date equipment. It is his impression that the equipment provided in vocational-technical institutions is "ten years out-of-date." He referred to the use of computers for drafting rather than drawing boards, and he looks for "tremendous change" in equipment manufacturing. He proposes that there be more internships, people training on the machines, then returning to the schools, and has offered 50 places in his plant where the local community college can provide hands-on-experience for an associate degree program. He sees the need, too, for faculty to be brought into industry for a period of time so that they can be kept up-to-date on the most modern equipment and have a feel for what is happening in industry.

Community colleges can often expand their physical plant resources greatly by utilization of "clinical settings." In one district the college works with 55 hospitals in health related programs. In the opinion of a college trustee, "We couldn't possibly duplicate that equipment and we also save capital."

Another college has an agreement with the county for joint use of recreational facilities at the college and in the parks. And the same arrangement will be applied for use of an auditorium which is to be built jointly by county and college.

Community agencies, business, industry, and the labor unions all have budgets, staff, facilities, boards and advisory groups, and very often funds designated for education and training. All of these represent potential resources for educational programs.

Obstacles to Cooperation

It's easy to talk about coordination and cooperation but it may be a different matter to bring it about. Financial pressures appear to accentuate competitive tendencies. Institutions become more aggressive in justifying themselves, often at the expense of others. For example, declining enrollments in public schools seem to step up the interests of school leaders in the field of adult education. And the community college may be seen as an interloper, poaching on a territory staked out by the public schools in an earlier period. Much the same could be said about the field of vocational education. Now, more than half of all community college students are enrolled in vocational-technical programs. This was not the case 15 years ago. At that time the colleges seemed preoccupied with the preparation of young people to transfer to four-year colleges. In the intervening period, not only have more students sought occupational objectives, but much of vocational education has moved beyond the secondary school to the postsecondary levels—which happens to be the same arena occupied by the community colleges. Hence, vocational educators may see the college as competitor or even adversary.

Sentimental appeals to collaboration and cooperation are seldom effective, at least not for long. There must be a quid pro quo. The advantages of cooperation must be made clear. In a report by the Board of Higher Education in Illinois, it was put this way: "There is a fine line between cooperation and competition—cooperation occurs when the advantages gained by all parties outweigh what each must sacrifice in order to participate in a joint venture. Competition will often occur when the reverse is true."[3]

"The advantages of cooperation" have generally not been "made clear" with regard to patterns of financial support in the various states. Student-based formulas do not promote the efforts required to develop liaison or to provide for continuing assessment of educational needs and interests. Seldom is the time (support money) provided for staff and faculty of the college to work with other community agencies and organizations. "These contacts out in the community don't count toward the work load," it is said. On the other hand, many institutions are now developing contractual arrangements that include the cost of developmental activities. But who does this and how well are they prepared for tasks that probably were not envisioned in graduate school programs? An administrator says:

> As we work with an increasing number of other organizations in the community, local, state and federal agencies, as we engage in consortium type activities, we're going to have to learn the knack of doing that. We have to learn how to work with these people without their organizations really dominating us.

And a chancellor had similar concerns:

> We don't have the talent for this kind of work in our institutions now or the resources. Our people aren't really trained to work with CETA and to negotiate center contracts. If we don't do it right then we are open to charges of mismanagement and these days you don't have the resources to afford mistakes. Also we have many pressures on us to cut down on management costs.

On the other hand, faculty who are interested in more community relationships offer this view: "The college administration is accustomed to traditional classroom roles and they don't provide time for inter-organizational relations, nor travel expense."

Other difficulties reported in relating to the organizational world off campus are what are perceived to be "vested interests." Said one president:

> The biggest problem in working in this area of public services is the little empires you have to deal with—the organizational entities in the area. The firemen are even more difficult to work with than the nurses. So far we have not been able to work things out with the firemen the way we have with the law enforcement personnel. I may need to go public on this so that there would be community pressure to have them work with us.

The problems in organizational cooperation are real. The concept is still relatively new. Policy structures do not often facilitate on-going relationships. For many educational personnel the assignments are markedly different from what they were prepared to do in their professional training. But with all of that, the necessity for new partnerships is self-evident, the policy directions are beginning to appear, and the major questions over the next several years will not deal with whether community colleges and other community agencies and institutions will relate in their educational services but how this can best be done.

Policy for Cooperation

Policy proposals to affect cooperation and coordination in provision of opportunity for community-based lifelong education are heard with increasing frequency. At an Assembly in early 1979, sponsored by the American Association of Community and Junior Colleges, one hundred leaders of education, the media, labor, business, government and the foundations met to consider policies for lifelong education. Among their recommendations are a number of references to cooperative effort:

- That community colleges join with other community organizations to sponsor local assessments and other activities that will result in a current picture of unmet lifelong educational needs. Implicit in this recommendation is the belief that community colleges can work with other organizations to solve social problems. . . .

- That such assessments of needs then be translated into statements of priorities that can be used by policy makers. The statement of needs and priorities should be developed in cooperation with interested community organizations. The interested organizations should unite in presenting their statements of needs and priorities to local, state, and federal funding sources, as well as to business, unions, foundations, and other private agencies that can provide support.
- That community colleges cooperate with other community agencies to conduct hearings on lifelong education and how to best meet identified needs . . .
- That community colleges collaborate with other community agencies to define the clientele to be served through lifelong education, to shape educational programs to meet consumer needs, and to provide access for all clientele into appropriate programs.
- That college presidents take the initiative in bringing together community representatives from all organizations and institutions which provide lifelong education experiences and that the various groups join together to sponsor a community educational information center. The information center would offer educational brokering services information on various resources, as well as counseling and referral services . . .
- That the AACJC sponsor a ''National Issues Forum'' as a model for a series of community forums on lifelong education. And that the AACJC community forums mechanism involve institutions, museums, businesses, industries, labor, and other institutions of higher education plus other schools and agencies presently performing an educational function.
- That an ''Urban Extension Act'' be enacted to provide federal funding incentives for the development of urban extension programs similar to the rural cooperative extension program. The resources of city governments and institutions of postsecondary education should be utilized cooperatively in meeting the lifelong education needs of urban citizens.[4]

Master Plan in Illinois

A step that is closer to the level of policy enactment was the adoption by the Illinois Community College Board of a 1979 Statewide Master Plan which projects developments in that state over the next five years. The Plan cites an educational program which will have excellent potential for further development during the next five years: ''Increased use of cooperative educational arrangements with the other community colleges, private technical schools, four-year colleges and universities and other agencies such as CETA.''

Goals Statement in New York

Excerpts from a common goals statement adopted by the Futures Committee of the New York State Advisory Council on Adult Learning Services illustrate other elements in the theme of collaboration. Presented is the concept of a lifelong learning system which necessarily brings together institutions that have often been relatively self-contained. Also acknowledged is the necessity for a broad panoply of services to match diversity in the population. And the importance of choice is recognized, which leads one to question whether cooperation and coordination imply the total elimination of duplicative services. The New York statement suggests some values in not pushing coordination and "efficiency" toward monopoly:

1. Learning services for adults in New York State are provided as an element of a lifelong learning system which integrates the previously separate systems: K–12, postesecondary and adult.
2. Learning services are available to the total population and are responsive to the diverse and emerging needs of adults with cultural, economic, physical, intellectual and other differences.
3. To promote quality and responsive services, adults are free to choose among diverse and possibly competing providers.
4. Learning services are provided at times, at places and for a time duration that responds to learner needs.
5. Information and guidance concerning learning services are readily accessible to all.[5]

Coordination in Florida

Policy has already been enacted in the State of Florida "to encourage the development of needed offerings . . . and to avoid unwarranted duplications." Coordinating councils are required by the legislature to relate vocational education, adult general education, and community instructional services. Here are some of Florida's administrative rules:

> A coordinating council for vocational education, adult general education, and community instructional services shall be established in each community college district. The membership of this council shall include the superintendent and directors of vocational education and adult general education of each school district in the community college area and the president and deans or directors of vocational education and community instructional services of the community college.

(1) The council shall develop recommendations to the respective school boards and to the community college board of trustees and where appropriate may make recommendations to the commissioner and to the appropriate division directors of the department.

(2) The responsibilities of the council shall be to review the total vocational education, adult general education, and community instructional services programs being offered in the district, to make such recommendations as are necessary, to encourage the development of needed offerings or changes in existing offerings and to avoid unwarranted duplications. To accomplish this, the council should perform the following:

(a) Review and recommend adjustments of existing programs, activities, and services—including counseling that will better meet the assigned responsibilities of each district;

(b) Review and recommend agreements between boards, to provide coordinated and articulated vocational education, adult general education, and community instructional services programs to meet the educational needs of all residents in all communities in the district;

(c) Review and make recommendations concerning long-range (6 years) objectives for the school district and the community college area of responsibility and make such recommendations as needed so that each plan provides for coordinated and articulated programs without unnecessary duplication;

(d) Review data in support of proposed programs, recommend to the appropriate board approval or disapproval of the program and, if necessary, recommend the assignment of responsibility to the appropriate institution in accordance with specific local cooperative agreements and rules of the State Board; and

(e) Review such other aspects of the programs and make such recommendations as are necessary to provide efficient, well-coordinated, and comprehensive vocational education, adult general education, and community instructional services programs.

(f) Individual boards shall consider recommendations of this council in taking action on matters included in paragraphs (2), (b) and (c) above.[6]

Conversations with administrators and trustees leave the impression that in some of the districts the process is working well, but that in others, particularly in multi-county districts, there are competing interests whose differences are not readily being accommodated. In spite of the problems that may exist at the district level, however, administrators suggest that it is essential to work out issues of coordination there rather than to buck them up to the state. The state provides powerful motivation for reconciliation of differences through a requirement that, before funds are released, a proposed program of coordinated effort be submitted to the State Commissioner of Education for approval.

Voluntary Coordination

Coordination can be voluntary. There is some evidence to suggest that if it is not voluntary it may soon be mandated by those bodies that appropriate funds. Rochester, New York, offers an example of how a number of different kinds of community organizations can join forces. In that area a consortium of business, industry, government, and higher education has been established to identify urban problems and to indicate where higher education can provide help in solving them. Initiative for its establishment came from within the community. Sponsoring organizations include the colleges and universities in the area, public broadcasting stations, commercial television, the Rochester Public Library, and the Rochester Museum and Science Center. Called the Urbanarium, the purpose of the incorporated organizations is to assist the community in identifying issues facing the greater Rochester area, provide an independent forum for clarifying policy alternatives, and to improve institutional capabilities for solving community problems. The Urbanarium acts primarily as a broker among community groups and agencies in the sponsoring educational, research, and communications institutions. It has developed informational materials on downtown development efforts, conducted volunteer and citizen participation training, and offered a workshop on regional government for leaders of the cities of Rochester and Syracuse. It was one of the sponsors of the Rochester Idea, a 1975 exhibition of citizen proposals for bettering the city.

According to the chairman of the Urbanarium, "educational institutions are facing greater demands for their services while at the same time the economic situation has forced them to operate under greater restraints. Cooperative efforts provide an effective and efficient way to expand the impact of these organizations in helping to maintain the vitality of the community. After all, the future of each institution is tied to helping the metropolitan area."

Education-Work Councils

It is often difficult to achieve voluntary or mandatory working relationships within the community. Some lessons have been learned about collaborative effort through the establishment of community education-work councils. In October 1976, the American Association of Community and Junior Colleges was awarded a contract by the United States Department of Labor to establish education-work councils in at least five local communities across the country. Local community colleges were to serve as council initiators. The council project was based on the belief that local communities are capable of identifying and addressing their own problems, that they are actively willing to assume such responsibilities, and that federal program support dollars are helpful in encouraging communities to focus on national issues as they are translated locally. The project was based upon the belief that individual community efforts may be more effective in resolving local problems than are expansive federal programs.

The program was based on the description presented in *The Boundless Resource*:

> Relying essentially on local community initiative, the councils would ferry people and ideas across the gap between education and employment and at the same time infuse the coming-of-age process with knowledge and experience available from the broader community. They would facilitate the transition of the younger members of the community between institutionalized education and whatever is to follow it, although without commitment to the one-way order of experience this suggests. This function would include both the rendering of services directly to youth and the ''brokering'' of functions of established institutions—particularly schools, employing enterprises, labor unions, employment agencies, and families.[7]

Among the reasons the Department of Labor viewed community colleges as logical local institutions to initiate councils were these: (1) They are community-based organizations responsible for servicing local educational needs and for anticipating future requirements; (2) They are generally governed by locally elected or appointed community leaders who often represent the variety of community components sought for membership on the councils.

James Mahoney, director of the AACJC program, reports that, as expected, the colleges were successful in attracting to the first meetings of the councils high-level individuals from government, organized labor, private industry, and other education institutions. However, Mahoney identifies some inter-organizational difficulties encountered even though the project experience suggested that community colleges are excellent resources for initiating and nurturing councils.

The seven counties making up one college service area carefully protected their jurisdictions. Most were hesitant to work with other counties on a program. They viewed their circumstances as different from others, were reluctant to discuss them with members from outside the county, and preferred to leave other county problems alone. One college, part of a statewide community college system, was frustrated by the restrictive, bureaucratic policies governing college operations. Travel requests, purchase orders, and staff hiring procedures took weeks to gain approval. Council responsiveness and flexibility were impeded.

"Collaboration," according to Mahoney, a central element in the council concept, "has a positive ring, but it caused no end of difficulty, confusion, and frustration." More specifically:

> While the term may be understandable on a theoretic level, its practical dimensions were never clear. The term assumes that community problems are the responsibility of the whole community, not the one or two organizations which are directly involved in a specific area. It implies that credit for achievement and blame for failure is spread community-wide. It suggests the active participation of all significant community components in the identification and resolution of problems, with no single component assuming more authority or control than any other. The term is often contrasted to the word "cooperation" which connotes most frequently the passive approval of one or more organizations for the work of another. Collaboration implies active participation in the analysis of problems, a readiness to provide specialized assistance and knowledge, and a willingness to offer resources helpful in resolving problems.[8]

Some councils did not evolve to a condition of full collaboration for various reasons. These include: a missing sense of program "ownership;" an incapacity to overcome the initial nebulousness of the project's purposes and characteristics; reluctance on the part of members to relinquish "territorial rights," both in terms of professional worlds and geographic ones; membership turn-over caused by community politics, job changes, professional and family commitments; fatigue; and the dominance of a single organization.

What Works?

What was learned from the development of education-work councils that might contribute toward the success of collaborative efforts by community organizations? The project reports that the greatest possibility for success lies with a group which would attempt to:

Realize practical results from their volunteered time as quickly as possible.

Actively participate (preferably in small task groups focusing on smaller, clearly delineated issues designed to meet council objectives) in identifying and resolving community problems; and

Attribute direct credit for council achievements and broadcast credit community-wide.

Other observations can be useful to those interested in advancing effective working relationships among community agencies and organizations. Clear and reasonable goals should be established early in the program. The goals should be the result of membership consensus and should be tailored specifically to community conditions. In establishing the goals, community officials who may not be able to participate on the council but who could contribute a great deal to facilitate the group's work—such as the mayor or other political leaders, directors of state government cabinet offices—should be invited to assist the council in its activity. Once the council's directions have been set, its presence, goals, planned activities and membership should be publicized throughout the community.[9]

State and Local Government

Mention mayors and other political leaders as well as the process of working with community agencies and the program which will probably first come to mind for community college administrators is CETA. The Comprehensive Employment and Training Act, with its decentralized approach through prime sponsors, created a "new ballgame" for many educators. The act is designed to provide "job training and employment opportunities for economically disadvantaged, unemployed and underemployed persons," to enable them to secure and retain self-sustaining, unsubsidized employment. It is administered nationally by the U.S. Department of Labor. The program is a very large one, currently operating under appropriations of $5.3 billion.

Administration is decentralized with state and local governmental units responsible for operating CETA employment and training programs to serve the needs of their communities. Programs desired by the sponsoring governmental units include classroom training, on-the-job training, work experience, counseling, testing, job development, and supportive services. Sponsors can arrange to provide these services directly or through contracts or sub-grants with education and training organizations. Representatives of educational institutions often find themselves on terrain new to them as they deal with governmental personnel at state and local levels, and particularly as they find it essential to work with organizations that represent the "target groups," that is, the members of the community who are unemployed, underemployed, and/or economically disadvantaged. Difficult though such initiatives might be, there is substantial motivation for educational institutions when they find that, if their institutions cannot adapt to meet the needs, other kinds of organizations will emerge to compete for funds and public support.

Community colleges have become leading actors in this field because of their placement in the community, their history of community service, and their existing relationships through advisory commitees and local boards of trustees. But it would be unwise to minimize the complexities experienced by the colleges in this important field of service. Political conditions and sophistication of college personnel both vary widely in. governmental jurisdictions throughout the country. Some community colleges have been able to relate effectively to the sponsors and target group organizations. Many have not. The point here is that CETA is a fact of life. Job training to deal with unemployment is of federal concern. Funds are available. They are routed through state and local governmental units. Community colleges are in the business of education and training. Those institutions that have brought their resources to bear upon the training needs have learned how to participate in the intricate governmental network.

Cooperation with Unions

Unions, business, and industry are developing new relationships with community colleges in education and training. Formerly the picture often appeared to be—"you train them and we'll use them." Advisory committees helped to keep programs current and to uncover job opportunities. Now some institutions have moved beyond that "producer-consumer" model to an association that tends to be continuous. The college services are considered an essential ingredient to the functioning of business, industry, and the labor unions.

"Education is the cornerstone of strength of any organization," testified Hazel P. Brown, president of the Harry Lundeberg School of Seamanship to the Senate Labor and Human Resources Committee at its hearings on "The Workplace and Higher Education."

President Brown represented the Seafarers International Union. All funds supporting the school which trains inland boatmen and unlicensed seafarers in the United States are obtained through the collective bargaining process. Thirty deep-sea companies and 100 towing companies contribute to the school through their contractual agreements with the SIU. The school offers college courses in cooperation with Charles County Community College. In fact, President Brown said that "the Lundeberg School has become a satellite program of the college." Further, she testified that "the local four-year liberal arts college had no interest in any form of liaison with a 'union' school. We, therefore, had to look to a community college in an adjacent county. The community college had the ability to be flexible in offering off-campus programs." [10] Although paying tribute to the cooperating community college, the representative of the Seafarers Union declared:

> Educational opportunities must be made readily accessible and more relevant to the worker, if he is going to have the option of achieving his potential through formal educational experiences. [11]

The late William Abbott, who directed AACJC's Service Center for College-Labor Union Cooperation, reported that unionists point to "academic arrogance" as a vice which deeply disturbs blue collar workers.

> Academics, they say, insist that workers, already tired from a full day's work, battle traffic and parking to go to a campus at convenient times for the teachers, not for the students. Colleges also present packaged courses or programs to workers instead of letting the workers determine what they want to learn. Professors lecture instead of discuss, and then wonder why workers walk out on them . . . On many campuses there is simply no place for a worker to feel at home . . . Although unionists point out that our system of free public education was born of union agitation in the 1830's. [12]

However, surveys by Abbott indicated that the picture is changing. There are 1200 apprenticeship training programs on community college campuses. Some colleges have branch campuses at the union headquarters. Union retirees go to college for a variety of reasons. Several trends are suggested:

> The most significant one appears to be that of labor, management, and education combining in the interest of social improvement. To save jobs in the case of Jamestown, New York. To save a city

overrun with violence and decay in Oakland, California. To help young people train for existing jobs, as in the case of community education work councils scattered throughout the country. These labor-management-education committees are mushrooming because education is the key to the changing work picture. Training is one area where labor and management are often in agreement. There is no reason not to work together and every reason to collaborate.[13]

In Economic Development

Gaining momentum rapidly in several states is a related development, the utilization of community colleges as a resource by a state interested in economic growth and in attracting business and industry from other states and countries. The State of South Carolina declares to national and international business and industrial interests:

> Traditionally, manufacturers expend much time and money to recruit and train a work force for a new plant. These and other costs result in huge start-up losses which force the new plant to operate in the red far too long. This practice is not only wasteful, it's unnecessary . . . at least, it's unnecessary in South Carolina . . . The Division of Industrial and Economic Development of the State Technical Education System stands ready to ensure your industry of the trained employees necessary for a profitable operation from plant start-up.[14]

Florida is doing this. Perhaps it is not just the sun which is attracting more business and industry to the southeastern states— The Utility Power Corporation under its two parent corporations, one in Germany, and Allis Chalmers of Milwaukee, recently built its new $150 million plant in Florida. Among reasons for locating there was ". . . the continuing support of the community, the city, the county, and state government agencies, and *especially your excellent training facilities.*"

Increasingly, community colleges are developing courses tailored to the specific needs of industries, businesses, and agencies within their geographical areas. Frequently these courses are developed on a contractual basis with the firm desiring the educational services. The course content will be adapted to the specific requirements of the firm and its employees. The entire course may be purchased at an agreed-upon cost or employees may be sponsored by their companies or unions in regular on-going courses.

In Battle Creek, Michigan, where there has been high unemployment for some years, there is a vigorous program to develop an 1800-acre industrial park and to attract industry from other parts of the world. Battle Creek Unlimited, the marketing organization for the industrial park, reponds to inquiries about utilities, land, and manpower by providing materials that describe the combined resources of Kellogg Community College and Calhoun Area Vocational Center. These two institutions jointly publish a brochure, "A Shared Program Between Educational Institutions for the Preparation and Upgrading of Skilled Personnel." A flow chart shows how employees may coordinate with educational institutions to fulfill their needs for skilled employees, beginning with a recognized employment need, moving them to special training required.

With Vocational Institutions

The cooperative stance of the community college and the area vocational center reflects another change that is taking place in institutional relationships. Little more than "lip service" was being paid to local coordination and common planning among area vocational schools and community colleges, David Bushnell reported following a study he completed in 1974. These institutions have often met on the battlefield of financial allocations. Now serious efforts are under way to develop practices and procedures that lead to better service for students, often at less cost, by fostering cooperative relationships at the local level.

Kellogg Community College and Calhoun Area Vocational Center actually began their relationship with the study that led to the establishment of the center. College land adjoining the campus was made available to build the center, bringing the two institutions physically closer together. In fact, the school and the college entered into a contractual arrangement to share facilities. Where advance courses at the high school or the vocational institution overlap with the introductory courses at Kellogg Community College, an agreement for a joint effort has been obtained. Students may receive college recognition for the course. KCC's learning resource center has opened its production service facilities to the vocational center. They cooperate in operating an adult skill center in the evening open to adults and involving the Urban League, Michigan Employment Security Commission, CETA, and a community action agency. The College also offers its services to area schools in community education programs. Out of this initiative has grown a common registration date for all, common class listings, a joint newspaper and radio advertising campaign, and a cooperative student referral service. This means that a student can go to one community education center and register for classes in any of the 18 centers. Those involved testified that no one suffered from working in harmony instead of competition. Rather, enrollments and services have tripled over this period of cooperation, and the people working with it say this is the power of synergism at work, that is, the effect together is greater than the sum of the individuals.

Proximity and Cooperation

Proximity of location may facilitate working relationships between institutions, though there are well-known cases of institutions separated by only a street where each is apparently oblivious of the existence of the other. According to the state superintendent in Illinois, policy determinations were made in that state some years ago that resulted in vocational high schools now being located usually on the same site as community colleges where they can share facilities. In his opinion, this is an excellent arrangement and it is a mistake to build the institutions so far apart that cooperation is impaired.

A number of the upper-division universities in Florida (they have no freshmen and sophomore courses) and community colleges are making space arrangements designed to promote liaison. Palm Beach Junior College operates a center on the campus of Florida Atlantic University at Boca Raton. Ten acres of the University campus have been turned over to the junior college for construction of facilities to be used for community college programs. And, jointly with the university, it is planned to erect a building on the North Campus of the junior college which will be the locale of university programs. Just a few hundred yards away from the campus of Gulf Coast Community College, West Florida University, another upper-division institution, will be building new facilities. Already a number of cooperative measures are in effect between the two institutions.

With Health Agencies

The move toward collaborative relationships is under way in a number of promising directions. One of the most fruitful partnerships appears to be that of education and health. In Baltimore County, Maryland, Essex Community College shares a 240-acre campus with Franklin Square Hospital (a private non-profit, non-sectarian community hospital) and the Baltimore County Health Department. A formal organization was established in July, 1973, to ensure that the three institutions coordinate their resources and services to provide high quality and comprehensive health and education services to the community. Each institution provides one-third of the operational support for a core staff and one-third of the membership to the governing body, the board of directors.

Vernon Wanty, president of Essex Community College and of the Health and Education Council, reports that:

> Through the efforts of the Health and Education Council, the College has had the unique opportunity of participating in the design and delivery of health services. For example, the Council implemented a cervical cancer screening program combining resources from the three institutions. The College supplied physician assistant students to perform the pap smears, and nursing students to do hypertension screening and self breast examinations. These resources, working in conjunction with physicians from Franklin Square Hospital and public health nurses of the Baltimore County Health Department, were able to screen as many women in a six-week period in our area as were screened throughout the entire State of Maryland over a nine-month period.
>
> We have found that the Council has very talented multidisciplinary staff possessing expertise not ordinarily found in community-based institutions. Accordingly, each institution has from time to time used this staff to assist in discharging various duties of a highly technical nature.

With assistance from the W. K. Kellogg Foundation, the council has established a Community Center for Continuing Education. The center provides continuing education in all health care disciplines with emphasis upon primary care.

Joint Use of Space

There are numerous examples of community colleges and other city agencies that have joined in the use of space. In the St. Petersburg Junior College District the college will provide the building for the new Clearwater Library, and the library will provide books and personnel under an arrangement for joint use. The city and the college, under a similar agreement, share in the use of a baseball field, tennis courts, and computers. Instances of this type are becoming more common and suggest that, for purposes of economy and promotion of greater participation, developments along these lines in Europe be studied. In a number of areas it is not unusual to find community schools, medical centers, recreation facilities, and expanded resource libraries built contiguously in shopping centers.[15]

Interfusion of educational services and resources into other community places and programs is well illustrated in the United States by Coastline Community College in southern California. Instruction is offered in 127 locations, including neighborhood schools, churches, commercial business buildings, civic buildings, community clubhouses, and senior citizen centers. Instruction is also offered by broadcast television, video tape and newspapers, telephone, and by mail. The college bookstore is located in a shopping center in the center of the district. In a three-year period, since its opening, almost 130,000 students attended Coastline.

Community Forums

One of the most productive vehicles in the forging of organizational relationships during the past few years has been that of the community forums initiated by community colleges. In recognition of the need for broad and informed participation in the shaping of public policies, the colleges have joined with numerous other community organizations and agencies to sponsor informed discussion of such issues as inflation, increased health costs, rising crime rates, pollution of air and water, and the developing energy crisis. In forums on "Crime and Justice" in a Florida community, there were more than 40 co-sponsors, ranging from TV stations and newspapers to the county sheriff's department, other colleges and universities, the court system, Chamber of Commerce, public library system, and the League of Women Voters, among others. The discussions were lively, well-attended, and successful in every way. It is now clear that one of the greatest benefits growing out of the community forums in that Florida county was the initiation of a network of communication and interaction among a large number of organizations and agencies, the work of which bears on the quality of community life. There is evidence that the relationships thus formed are continuing.

In early 1980, 12 national organizations participated in a nationwide public discussion program, "Energy and the Way We Live," via "community forums" and "town meetings" with leadership from community colleges. Those organizations have their extensions and counterparts at the community level and represent a good sample of the kinds of groups the colleges will be associated with as they "encourage and facilitate lifelong learning with community as process and product." The list includes:

Courses by Newspaper
WTBS-Television
American Library Association
National Association for Advancement of Colored People
Rural America, Inc.
Foreign Policy Association
United Church Board for Homeland Ministries

National Public Radio
American Association of Museums
The Rene Dubos Forum
National Wildlife Federation
Federation of Public Programs in the Humanities

In Telecommunications

In the facilitation of lifelong learning in the community, no partnership offers more potential than that of the community college and organizations in telecommunications. Cable television, satellites, and videodiscs have the capacity to remove common obstacles to learning—distance, time, abstractness, lockstep routines, and high tuition. The country's public television stations are about to be satellite connected, and the Public Broadcasting Service is expressing new interest in national educational services. At an AACJC Assembly in late 1979, ways were explored to promote greater cooperation between community colleges and local television stations with the aim of making it possible to deliver broader educational options to adult learners. Recommendations called for improved policies at the local, state and federal levels, within both the public and private sectors, in order to build an environment more conducive to cooperation between the community college and broadcast communities.

CHANGE Magazine, in an editorial, noted:

> In higher education the only significant national initiatives in these areas have been those of the American Association of Community and Junior Colleges. It now exerts increasingly interesting leadership through a special task force on the uses of mass media in learning. Thanks to the close collaboration between the Public Broadcasting Service and several important community college production centers, over 100,000 Americans now take for credit telecourses through community college facilities.[16]

Notwithstanding significant accomplishments in this field, one has the feeling that a real partnership between educators and communications technologists can provide broader access to educational opportunity than we have dared to imagine. The Assembly called for improvement of the capacity of community and junior colleges to deliver instruction via new media by creating partnerships between colleges and television broadcasters at the local, regional, and national levels to serve adult learners in diverse ways. Also it was proposed that a special task force be formed, made up of representatives from community colleges and from telecommunications organizations "to seek solutions; to provide colleges and stations with advice, guidance, and assistance to help them solve these problems, and to represent both parties' special and unique interests before the appropriate governmental bodies at the national level.'' [17]

Cooperative Arrangements

Other illustrations could be given of ways in which community colleges have tied into networks of other organizations with interests in education. A survey was conducted by AACJC to find out how many cooperative arrangements the colleges have with other organizations, agencies, and institutions in their communities in providing educational services. Fifty percent of the colleges replied. The average college reported 100 cooperative arrangements. Most of the arrangements were with business and industry. It was not unusual for the college representative to write in some comment to the effect: "We never realized how much of this we are doing until we pulled this information together to answer your questions."

Many other illustrations could be given of ways in which community institutions and organizations are relating their efforts. With all that is being done, though, the reports are still newsworthy, which suggests that the establishment of such relationships has not yet become a central objective in most community colleges.

Organization for Cooperation

By and large the organizational structure of the college does not reflect the importance of institutional liaison in the encouragement and facilitation of learning. Earlier it was reported that staff time was not often made available for this purpose. There are some exceptions. A few institutions now have "salesmen," "brokers," directors of "marketing," and coordinators whose responsibilities would include inter-organizational relationships in the community.

Clackamas Community College in Oregon has Community Development Coordinators to work "in cooperation and coordination with local, county, and state agencies and organizations which provide, or have the potential to provide, human services."[18] They are charged to establish cooperative relationships with agencies/organizations serving the community. The college wants these people to be highly visible in the community and prefers, therefore, not to house them on campus and prefers them to be members of the community in which they are working. The five coordinators are housed in a senior citizen center and local community schools offices. Their basic responsibility is to work with county, city, school districts and other agencies, public or private, to solve problems that have developed within the community.

The president of a Virginia community college describes his staff organization for relating to community services in the following table.

(The percentage figures represent the proportion of that individual's time allotted to planning, organizing, and operations. Note the large commitment to planning by the president. Most of this involves community relationships.)

Organization for Community-Based Education

	Strategic Development	Tactical Development	Operations-Administration
President	40%	30%	30%
Provost	20%	20%	60%
Director, Continuing Education	30%	40%	30%
Assistant Director		30%	70%
Program Head		20%	80%
Office of Community Development	50%	35%	15%

Organization of a California community college makes clear the high priority given to community relations. There are five offices—Office of Instruction; Admissions, Guidance and Information Services; Telecourse Design; Administrative Services; and *Community Activities (operating under the office of the President).* [19] The latter arrangement represents a quantum leap over the traditional concept of community service as usually the third in college program priorities.

The Most Important Factor

Another obvious lag in translating the concept of collaboration into practice is the policy framework within which institutions legally function, particularly with regard to the essential element of financial support. But perhaps more important than all other other factors in facilitating appropriate change is the view of community college leadership.

Several community college presidents were talking about change. Questions asked in the local newspapers about the role of their colleges seasoned the discussion. Their comments (expressed with feeling) were something like this:

> We bear the brunt of living on the horizon of education. The sixties were idealistic. We were idealistic. Now these are different times with a very practical approach to life. We succeeded in those days because of our numbers. We had limited space and we were forced into what seemed to be perceived as essential fields.

> Now, as we look ahead, we need to tie in with other efforts in the community. We need to find alliances in order to fulfill our mission. We're in a different kind of educational institution, a link between the world that produces knowledge and the community. We're filling gaps left by other institutions.

> The idea has been that we prepare people for this or that. But it is better to find people at work and then to work with them. Increasingly, we ought to move toward intern and co-op programs where people are already engaged in jobs that exist.

These presidents were grappling with something very fundamental. As they looked at their communities they did not see individual, unconnected, prospective students as much as they saw people at work in the community. People who were involved in civic activities, employed in offices and stores, factories and hospitals. People who played in orchestras and went to the museums and used the libraries and the recreation centers. People who watched television and read newspapers and listened to the radio. People who belonged to unions and Rotary Clubs and worked with YMCA and Boy Scouts and the churches, synagogues, and neighborhood associations. In fact, these presidents used the words clients and participants more often than the word students. They envisioned a society in action and, in effect, were asking how the community college ties in with organized community life. Schools often have been very close to family as an institution for primary relationships—essential in the process of socialization. In many communities the church has a similar role. But college has been something to go away to. Something spatially and psychologically distant. A community college, on the other hand, has some of the advantages of the schools (at their best). It can be perceived as part of the community, not strange or alien, particularly as it links into existing alignments or associations of people. As mentioned previously, the popular associations in Scandinavia—labor unions, conservation associations, temperance organizations—sponsor educational activities with remarkably high participation rates. There are good reasons for such involvement. People associate with others they know. They have trust in their organizations. They are learning on familiar ground.

There is a Japanese concept of marriage which may be useful to make the point. The Japanese find it difficult to understand our ways of courtship, especially the possibility that a man and a woman may decide to marry without their families ever having met. In Japan, a man or woman not only takes a wife or a husband but a family as well.

One of the great values in relating to other community agencies and organizations is the possibility that the college is acquiring an extended "family" of learners and providers of education, not merely an individual student.

The American Association of Community and Junior Colleges has drafted a mission statement and continuing objectives to give direction to Association activities for the next several years. The mission statement describes the Association as an organization for national leadership of lifelong education for individual and community development. One of the five major objectives set forth is: To encourage working relationships with other institutions and agencies having similar concerns for individual and community development.

[1] K. Patricia Cross. "Community College Students Today and Tomorrow." Address given to the Arizona Community College Board, Phoenix, Arizona, February 16, 1979.

[2] Gene I. Maeroff. "Fight on Illiteracy Found to Lag Badly." *New York Times,* September 9, 1979, p. 1.

[3] "The End of Growth: Ramification for Higher Education Planning and Policy." Staff report presented to the Illinois Board of Higher Education, November 1, 1977. *The Illinois Trustee.* Educational Supplement, December 1977.

[4] Jamison Gilder, editor. *Policies for Lifelong Education, Report of the 1979 Assembly.* Washington, D.C.: American Association of Community and Junior Colleges, 1979.

[5] New York State Education Department, Adult Learning Services Advisory Council. "Common Goal Statement" (Unpublished). Albany: the Department, January 1979.

[6] Florida State Board of Education. *Administrative Rules for the Operation of Florida's Community/Junior Colleges.* Supplement No. 88. Tallahassee: the Board, 1978.

[7] Willard Wirtz. *The Boundless Resource.* Washington, D.C.: The New Republic Book Company, Inc., 1975.

[8] James R. Mahoney. *Community Education-Work Councils: The AACJC Project, Second Year. Summary and Analysis.* Washington, D.C.: American Association of Community and Junior Colleges, 1979, p. 4.

[9] Ibid. p. 10.

[10] Hazel P. Brown. "Labor Unions, Collective Bargaining and the Workplace." Testimony before Senate Labor and Human Resources Committee's Comprehensive Oversight Hearings on "The Workplace and Higher Education: Perspectives for the Coming Decade," June 1979.

[11] Ibid. p. 8.

[12] William Abbott. Unpublished material, 1978.

[13] Ibid.

[14] South Carolina State Board for Technical and Comprehensive Education. "Start Up in the Black in South Carolina." Brochure. Columbia: the Board.

[15] Educational Facilities Laboratories. *EFL Report*, No. 29. New York: the Laboratories, September 1978.

[16] "Education and the Telefuture." (Editorial) *Change*, November-December 1979, pp. 12-13.

[17] Marilyn Kressel, editor. *Adult Learning and Public Broadcasting*. Washington, D.C.: American Association of Community and Junior Colleges, 1980.

[18] Marvin Weiss. "The Sixth Dimension: Community Development." Memorandum, Clackamas Community College, December 1978.

[19] Coastline Community College. "Fact Sheet '79." Coastline Community College, October 1979, p. 2.

Chapter IV

COMMUNITY COLLEGES IN A POLICY FOR LIFELONG LEARNING

I have a friend and professional colleague with a positive and contagious outlook on life's happenings. Suppose a slowdown in operations by air traffic controllers delays his flight by four or five hours. His response will probably be something like this. "What luck! I've just started a good book and now I have several unanticipated hours for reading."

Someone has said that an adventure is an inconvenience rightly perceived. What do we see in community college developments? What is the meaning of change in the institutions? Do the signals point toward inconvenience or adventure?

Community college personnel frequently express concern about the broad diversity of learners. There are "kids" of sixteen and other people old enough to be their grandparents. There are people on welfare and those who drive Porsches. Most of the students or learners are described as part-time. (A term of limited usefulness when it represents the norm.) And the learners seem to come and go and come again. Many maintain relationships with the college for a number of years as their interests and conditions of life develop. Some faculty and administrators recall with fond nostalgia the campus setting of their own academic experiences, a college community somewhat apart from the vicissitudes of contemporary society. The community college they view to be in and of the world. Community change and community concerns wash like waves through the college programs and structures. They ebb and flow. "Too bad!" say some academicians. "What luck!" say others.

Trends Toward Lifelong Education

Those with the positive outlook have remarkably strong arguments on their side. For institutional characteristics, often viewed as disadvantages by college personnel and policy makers, are cited by interpreters of lifelong education as significant features of what is likely to be the next major development in educational policy.

Education will be concurrent with the conduct of other responsibilities of adulthood. For most community college learners this is already the case. In many colleges, enrollees now span the generations, another important element in lifelong education. And community colleges relate to schools, places of work, culture and recreation, religious institutions, and mass media, a further mark of education that operates in the life-space of the individual and for the entire life span.

There is mounting evidence, then, that several trend lines in the evolution of community colleges lead toward the concept of lifelong education, now being adopted as a major guiding principle for reviewing and reconstructing educational systems in various parts of the world. In time, perhaps sooner than we now think, the United States will acknowledge the truth of Paul Lengrand's assertion, "the notion that a man can accomplish his lifespan with a given set of intellectual and technical luggage is fast disappearing."[1] Community colleges, because of characteristics that they have developed thus far, are in an advantageous position to build further on what are appropriate structures and to be in the vanguard of necessary change in policies, institutional forms, and citizen attitudes. Let it be said again, though, that crucial to that process is the capability of community college leadership to see that what have been perceived often as institutional encumbrances in truth can be bridges into a new era of education and community service.

A New Era

In that new era, education will be viewed as a continuing process throughout life and policy provisions now generally limited to children and youth will include entitlement of adults to appropriate education. For this to happen, a much better understanding is required both of the need for lifelong education and the nature of lifelong education. Although voluminous materials on the subject are now available, their translation into constructive discussion and policy development has been somewhat limited. However, two books produced by UNESCO during the 1970's are especially useful to describe deficiencies in current educational practices and to point toward more appropriate education for "the radically changing modern world."

Learning to Be, often called the Faure report, is a landmark statement on educational policy issued by UNESCO in 1972.[2] The sense of the book is reflected in the following paragraphs:

> . . . the commission laid stress above all on two fundamental ideas: lifelong education and the learning society. Since studies can no longer constitute a definitive "whole" handed out to and received by a student before he embarks on adult life, whatever the level of his intellectual equipment and the age at which he does so, our educational systems must be thought out afresh, in their entirety, as must our very conception of them. If all that has to be learned must be continually reinvented and renewed, then teaching becomes education and, more and more, learning. If learning involves all of one's life, in the sense of both time-span and diversity, and all of society, including its social and economic as well as its educational resources, then we must go even further than the necessary overhaul of "educational systems" until we reach the stage of a learning society. For these are the true proportions of the challenge education will be facing in the future. It is by no means certain that conservatism of a cultural nature will be easier to overcome than economic or political resistance. But once in position to measure the stakes against the price, how can we refuse to fight the fight?

> . . . There are immense possibilities for mass participation in the social and educational enterprise. Peoples until now submerged by the tides of history are becoming aware of their will and their power The size and strength of the potential to be unleashed through mobilizing the people, through volunteer movements and spontaneous popular organizations, is clear from examples in many countries over the past fifty years.

Liberating the energies of the people, unleashing their creative power, heads the list of future prospects for the development of education in the world of tomorrow.

Foundations for Lifelong Education

Other references were made in Chapter 1 to the point of view expressed in this powerful social document. In 1972, it was determined that the UNESCO Institute for Education should focus its international cooperative research program on "the content of education in the perspective of lifelong learning." One of the challenges, of course, is how to translate concepts into action. How does the concept of lifelong education become functional and effective? An important step was "to acquire an increasing degree of clarity and depth in our understanding of the ideal of lifelong education and its multiple implications with the help of a number of relevant disciplines of knowledge." Under the leadership of R. H. Dave, an interdisciplinary study team examined issues in the field with the help of accumulated knowledge represented in their disciplines. They tackled such questions as "Why should education be treated as a lifelong process? When it is so treated, what are the new roles and responsibilities that the field of education should assume? How far is lifelong education, in its new perspective, feasible and practical in different socio-economic and ideological conditions? What are the obstacles?"

Members of the team were from the fields of philosophy, history, economics, sociology, psychology, anthropology and ecology. The experts were requested to provide perspectives and guidelines from the standpoints of their respective disciplines to aim at establishing a knowledge base that could be useful in decision making as concepts of lifelong education are considered in the policy making process.

The working description of lifelong education utilized by the team will be helpful to us as we consider the part played by community colleges:

> Lifelong education is a process of accomplishing personal, social and professional development throughout the life-span of individuals in order to enhance the quality of life of both individuals and their collectives. It is a comprehensive and unifying idea which includes formal, non-formal and informal learning for acquiring and enhancing enlightenment so as to attain the fullest possible development

in different stages and domains of life. It is connected with both individual growth and social progress. That is why ideas such as "learning to be" and "a learning society" or "an educative society" are associated with this concept.[3]

In no way can justice be done here to the thoughtful and provocative synthesis of the research team. However, it will be helpful to use some of their perspectives as prisms through which to view and to consider community college movements toward a policy for lifelong education. The purpose here is to examine community college developments against a background of concepts.

"What is needed is an educational organization in which all citizens have access to education at a time when they feel the need of such access, and under circumstances in which they find the experience congenial and stimulating." [4]

A community college president asked, "Are we serving as holding tanks for people? People seem to wander through college." A board member raised questions about compulsory education and whether it is really good social policy to think in terms of compulsory education to age 18 or to when a person completes high school. "Are there not perhaps more beneficial ways in which many young people could be spending those developmental years? Maybe we are really doing a disservice to say that the only place to be in at this time in a person's life is the school."

The Carnegie Council on Policy Studies in Higher Education agrees. Its recommendations in late 1979 included an emphasis upon options:

> Make age 16 the age of free choice to leave school, take a job, enter the military service, enter other forms of service, continue in school, enter college, enter an apprenticeship. In particular, we see no clear need for compulsory attendance in school after age 16. At age 21, young persons should be as fully on their own as possible. Special help and the sense of dependency it fosters should not go on indefinitely.[5]

In broadening the choices of youth, the Council sees an important service function for community colleges:

> It would involve being available to all youths in the community to advise on academic and occupational opportunities, to offer job preparation classes, to make job placements, to work out individual

combinations of employment opportunities, to make referrals to CETA employers, to make referrals to sources of legal and medical advice, to refer to and to create apprenticeship programs. Additional and specialized personnel will be required for this purpose. These might be known as "youth service functions." Youths would be given an institutional base of operations.[6]

What should be one of the most apparent facts of life, individual differences, requires broader acknowledgment in educational policies and programs.

A young man, age 27, a student in a community college, was asked what learners should be given priority if the college could not take all applicants. He quickly replied, "Those age 30 or beyond. They need to get the education now that they didn't get earlier. This would not only benefit them but their children and society as well." He felt that his two small children would benefit from his own educational experiences. He was a high school "drop out." I asked why. He replied:

> I couldn't put up with the administration of the high school. Instead of the teachers concerning themselves with teaching mathematics, it was whether I was wearing socks. I quit, but then I took the GED. At the college here academics are prime and I don't have to fight the administration.

He was an honor student majoring in math education.

Students at a community college which emphasizes specialized technical programs spoke to the need for educational programs that make sense for them at a particular time in their own development.

A woman who has children ages 10 and 13 said that she went to college earlier because that was the thing to do. You go to college and you raise the kids. Now she realizes she can build a second career, a second life. Her view toward herself as a woman, she said, had changed. She had given 12 years to community service while the children were growing up. She was apprehensive when she started preparing for a new career. Many women like herself, she said, are fearful of the unknown. Yet, many of them, surmounting their fears, are turning to institutions like these (community colleges) to get ready for new pursuits.

Someone else said, "I am here to change careers. That's important to me and the college is providing that opportunity."

Another "student" with two children, one 15 and another 22, suggested that we are moving toward the concept of what he called incremental education. Even at this point, he reported, his children have attitudes toward education that are different from those he nourished as a younger person. He thinks people are willing to devote smaller portions of their time to education, but may be moving in and out of education, again and again, throughout their lives. So this kind of institution, he asserted, needs to be available and to accommodate to new educational life styles that may involve experiences over smaller periods of time. "There's no time at which you can stop and say you are educated. The mission is over a person's lifetime."

Developmental Stages

Some years ago in speaking to a group in Florida, I called for the development of what I termed a lifelong curriculum—I meant an organized system of learning experiences related to the different stages we pass through as we live our lives. Gail Sheehy in her book, *Passages*, elaborates very helpfully on that theme.

> If I've been convinced by one idea in the course of collecting all the life stories that form this book, it is this: Times of crisis, of disruption or constructive change, are not only predictable but desirable. They mean growth.

> The mystics and the poets always get there first. Shakespeare tried to tell us that man lives through seven stages in the "All the world's a stage" speech in *As You Like It*. And many centuries before Shakespeare, the Hindu scriptures of India described four distinct life stages, each calling for its own fresh response: student, householder, retirement when the individual was encouraged to become a pilgrim and begin his true education as an adult; and the final stage of sannyasin, defined as "one who neither hates nor loves anything."[7]

She describes the developmental ladder as having these rungs: "Pulling Up Roots"; "the Trying Twenties"; "Catch-30"; "Rooting and Extending"; "The Deadline Decade"; "Renewal or Resignation."

While I was trying to match these changes in the lives of people with the changes in tasks that people would be required to perform, I ran across a very stimulating approach which did exactly what I had been seeking. Vivian R. McCoy described seven developmental stages, beginning at age 18, with the seventh stage somewhat open-ended, but having its beginning point at age 65. She specified the tasks and illustrated the program response for those seven stages. And the essence of this point of view (see Appendix II):

> As an individual moves through the stages of adulthood, each stage confronts the person with central developmental tasks. Mastery of the tasks means progress for the individual; denial spells regression and difficulty with later tasks which build on previous mastery. The challenge to adult educators is to provide the learning necessary for adults to handle these life tasks. An educational advantage is the "teachable moment" which a developmental task typically signals in the learner.[8]

Those whose calling is education will see in life's "passages" or "developmental stages" two truths of profound significance. First, each stage of life requires learning to "handle those life tasks." And secondly, the learning process is facilitated as it relates to the required "developmental task." In other words, motivation exists. These can be "teachable moments."

However, the stereotype of educational need is still primarily of the child and youth. In reality, educational services should match all of the seven developmental stages—not just the first in adult life. Concentration of effort for the adult years as reflected in public policy in education has been on the "leaving home" group—ages 18–22. More attention has been given, for example, to the task of choosing a career than to subsequent stages, such as progressing in career, reexamining one's work life, adjusting to the realities of work, preparing for retirement and expanding avocational interests, disengaging from paid work to search for new achievement outlets. There are many factors in our environment now that indicate the probability that those later periods in the career cycle have both individual and social significance at least equal to career entry, and consequently calling for suitable educational services. It is important as well to recognize that the numbers of people in those age groups will proportionately increase.

Teachable Moments

As has been implied, the profile of learners participating in community colleges is changing to more nearly match the developmental stages—though there is a good distance to go in the later stages. If community colleges can learn how to relate well to those "teachable moments," a multiplying effect is possible. In what are usually short periods of contact with the college it would be possible to point the direction of attention toward learning opportunities that are available in a multitude of places in the community beyond the confines of the college. Some educational institutions have fostered a "dependency" trait in their clientele. If you want it, you must come here to get it. It's available nowhere else. We will decide how it is served and packaged. We will read it to you. We will tell you. Here is how you should do it. What if it were our aim, on the other hand, to promote in each of our clients as soon as possible the capacity to be self-propelled, self-directed, self-taught, and to be aware of the abundant aids to learning in his or her environment?

Both psychological and anthropological findings suggest that lifelong education is not only feasible, in that intellectual capacity persists throughout life, but that educational systems need to be coordinated to this rhythm of development in intellectual functioning.[9] The community college is responding through its open admissions stance, initiatives taken in relating to other community institutions, and flexibility in style, place, and time of services offered. However, deterrents do exist, and will be referred to in later chapters.

"There are grounds for believing that adults are perfectly capable of learning throughout life, and there are also grounds for believing that it is increasingly important that they actually do so." [10]

Large numbers of people beyond the conventional college age years are participating in educational activities. That fact has not been fully acknowledged in institutional plans, programs, and policies. A letter from a concerned president describes his discomfort at assumptions used for planning purposes:

> Recently I had the privilege of hearing Earl Cheit speak to the point of continuing change in the relationship between the state and higher education. During the presentation, attention was given to the question of changing enrollment patterns.

> Although most of the discussion was exceedingly relevant, when the enrollment question was addressed, I felt isolated as most community college presidents might. Projections cited are, or appear to be, based on the 18 to 21 or 24 age group exclusively. With a real life situation of a student body having an average age of 26 and only 30% of the students under 21 years of age, I must be skeptical about the general conclusions drawn regarding enrollment projection data through the 1980's.

The reason for my writing, then: Is there developed or being developed a set of data and projections reflecting the complete community college model of enrollments? Possibly I have missed some work or am revealing the thinness of my research, but nothing has been found in this area.

When I hear about the position taken by some state officials which appears to run counter to opportunities for lifelong learning, encounter limits imposed on degree enrollments, yet see people determined to grow in their jobs through the community college and meet senior citizens who want, hesitatingly, to take the opportunity they never had before, the strong need for an enrollment model that can be driven by some of these considerations arises. Without such a model and supportive data, I am unable to effectively communicate with key decision makers, board members, legislators, and state administrators. We can say that our enrollment pool is enormous but there seems to be little data to show precisely how various segments of the population have responded to us and how they might respond in the future.

Again, my question: Is there a good model available or is this something which requires considerable work, attention and funding?

My answer to his last question was, "Yes, considerable work is required," although in some areas there have been substantial changes in ways to project enrollments. For example, in some states postsecondary projections are now based on population aged 17 and over rather than "college-age." In a number of community college districts, estimates of future enrollments are related to a percentage of the total population of the district rather than the number of people in the immediate post-high school years (perhaps one out of seven or eight of population 17 and over). But there are many variables. One of the most crucial is that of what happens when our educational enterprise is built no longer on the assumption of a terminal point to education?

Leonard Woodcock, then president of the United Auto Workers, told the American Association of Community and Junior Colleges that the unions would be bringing educational enterprise to the bargaining tables.

We feel—or hope—that either the time has come or must come shortly when blue-collar and white-collar workers should benefit from the opportunity to break away from the daily grind without having to walk the bricks or stand in unemployment lines; that they should be free to go back to school, or up to college, or to write a book about the life of a worker, or whatever. Such workers, we believe, need to unwind, or renew their enthusiasm, or strike out in a new direction, or improve their skills as much as any college professor.[11]

Older Americans

And what of older Americans whose opportunities were limited 25 or 40 years ago when community colleges and similar institutions were not available? I am reminded of a statement by Samuel C. Brightman, director of education services for the National Council of Senior Citizens. He said the chairman of the appropriations committee of the House of the Arizona state legislature offered the opinion that retired people are merely using the college system as a place to go. "Those that are already retired, my God, they're using it as a hobby."

Brightman reports that the unpaid lobbyist for the Arizona Council of Senior Citizens made the following response to the legislator:

> . . . senior citizens resent the implication that there is nothing new or useful for older Americans to learn. Shouldn't we have the opportunity to improve our understanding and participation in the life of the community? The physical plants of the vast majority of colleges and universities in America were built by the taxes and contributions of those who are now senior citizens. Yet, as a group, they are the educationally deprived generation. One out of four never finished grade school, only one out of ten finished high school and probably one out of a hundred finished college. They now ask that the campuses they built admit them—without tuition.

Brightman amplifies the lobbyist's statement:

> . . . we entered the job market during the country's biggest depression and many of us started out with menial jobs at poor pay. We adopted Social Security . . . A good many of us found our way into combat zones in World War II and when we got back, we felt we were too old to use the GI Bill of Rights . . . We went back to working and paying taxes, and some of us still are. So I believe it is only simple equity to let us sample some of the free education we have provided for others.[12]

A community college trustee writing to another trustee about justification for education of older people maintains that the reasons for involving them are the same as those that justify provision of services for any other age group. "I do not think we need to find a new rationale to justify serving older Americans. Instead, we need to more clearly understand why the people who come to us for services do so."

He maintained that education combines with major changes in the life patterns of younger people to prepare them for the next stage of life. So it is with older persons.

> College then is a period in which through participation in classes, seminars, in social activities and study, the person builds a general knowledge of the world as it exists for him at that time and develops his own manner of coping with the world in which he finds himself, financially, socially, intellectually and romantically. His involvement in education fills his mind with possibilities and challenges him to chart a course for his personal immediate future. Persons in their sixties often find themselves in a situation which is almost identical. . .

Obsolescence

Another driving force toward adult learning is the threat of obsolescence. A UNESCO paper notes: "The increase in the volume of knowledge and the increasingly rapid obsolescence of what is learned make it impossible to restrict learning to the period of schooling, and compel the individual to supplement and renew his knowledge throughout his life. . ." [13]

Physicians have become aware of that need. Physicians registered under the American Board of Family Practice are required every seven years to stand for examinations which will test whether they are maintaining proficiency in their fields. Nineteen other medical groups are watching this development closely, with the likelihood that they will impose similar requirements.

In addition to the number seeking education to keep up in their fields, there are large numbers who want educational services to make it possible for them to change occupations. ". . . thirty six percent of the American population between the ages of 16 and 65 is in a career transition status." They are unemployed and looking for work or they are dissatisfied with a current job and considering a new career. Most adults in transition are presently employed and wish to either change fields, or to move to higher positions in their present fields. Most of those in transition recognize that the jobs they want may not be open or that they may lack the credentials and experience to qualify. So they are enrolling in educational institutions to upgrade their skills and to get new credentials.[14]

Adults without Formal Education

Many adults are not involved in educational activities. In Illinois there are some three million adults without high school diplomas. A report from New York State reveals that "nearly half of all adults in New York State have need of the basic educational and occupational skills which will enable them to cope with the demands of contemporary society." Further:

> According to the 1970 census, New York State had approximately 4.9 million adults aged 25 and older with less than a high school education. Of these adults, 2.9 million (59.1%) had eight years or fewer of formal education. These individuals as well as others served by the Division of Continuing Education make up 47% of the state's population and are classified as educationally disadvantaged . . . In order to participate these adults must overcome financial and personal barriers which currently limit their participation in these activities.[15]

Howard Bowen, distinguished educator-economist, who is of the opinion that for those who believe that higher education has already been overdone in the United States, points to surprising, sobering statistics that the educational attainments of the American people are meager even today. He also points out, however, that the situation is slowly being rectified in this generation:

> In the population 25 years of age and over there are about 119 million persons. Of them, about 25 millions have never been beyond grade school and another 18 millions have not completed high school. These two groups make up 36 percent, more than a third, of the population. At the other extreme, 33 millions, or just over a quarter, have attended college. But only 18 millions, fewer than 15 percent of the adult population, are college graduates.

Bowen says that if this is to be, indeed, a nation of educated people, there is need to increase the percentage of youths attending college and to enlarge the educational opportunities for adults beyond the usual college age. He says: "This is a task of all higher education, but it is especially the responsibility of the community colleges which are in a sense recruiters of new learners, both young and old. . ."[16]

The Dominant Function

Many adults are deeply interested in learning but want services that are informal, geared to their work or family schedules, readily available, practical, realistic, without the flavor of traditional schooling. Apparently some community colleges have been able to meet those conditions, for ''continuing education for part-time, adult students has become the dominant function of the community colleges'' in at least one large state, according to a significant study.[17]

The researcher, Dorothy Knoell, reports that the community college in California is no longer viewed as an extension of the secondary schools or as a ''junior'' higher education institution but as ''a uniquely community-based, postsecondary institution with the flexibility and resources to meet the needs of all kinds of adult students.''

Part-time students now comprise two-thirds of the headcount enrollment in the more than 100 community colleges of that state. They are described as:

> . . . older students who come with their own objectives relating to educational, career, and personal growth which often are achieved outside degree and certificate programs. They tend to enroll on an intermittent basis, that is, skipping semesters and enrolling in other institutions offering postsecondary programs. Although enrolled in courses offered for credit, they sometimes forego credits and grades on the grounds that they have no need for certification. Many already hold baccalaureate and advanced degrees but find courses in their local community colleges which satisfy a wide range of individual interests. . .[18]

Some consternation was caused by the Knoell report because convenient classification systems seemed to lose some credibility. Categories long relied upon—drop-out, attrition, transfer, degree-oriented—require fresh approaches to have any meaning in terms of a changing clientele.

State Policy

As we shall discuss in the next chapter, the legislative framework may not fit the realities of the community college picture. In some states, however, new policy statements recognize institutional change. North Carolina has developed a clear-cut statement. The Commission on Goals for the North Carolina Community College System, after examining state needs and projected trends, presented six goals for the large number of community colleges in that state. Note the specific references to "adult" population and to manpower development, accessibility, illiteracy, citizenship skills, a cultural renaissance, and use of resources:

1. To accelerate North Carolina's economic growth and development through a dynamic, responsive, relevant and comprehensive manpower training program.

2. To make education accessible to all North Carolina adults regardless of age, sex, socioeconomic status, or ethnic background.

3. To eliminate illiteracy among the adult population of North Carolina.

4. To enhance the development of effective citizenship skills among the state's adult population.

5. To promote and aid in the development of a cultural renaissance among the adult population of North Carolina.

6. To achieve excellence in the effective and efficient use of all human and material resources available to the North Carolina Community College System.

Evidence that adults are capable of learning throughout life and that it is increasingly important that they do so is impressive. Through an evolutionary process which accelerated over the past 10 years, community colleges find that they have become primarily a flexible educational resource for part-time adult students of all kinds.

What do we make of it? Students who are older, combining work and study, interested in a million different things, "dropping in" as family, job, and other obligations permit, resorting to the college as to the library as curiosity provokes and interest motivates. What do we make of it? How do we view what is happening?

America has unusual opportunities to build upon what is happening. Here there is no separate, self-contained enclave of education detached from the communities' life and problems—the kind of enclave which has brought violent revolution to societies less adaptable. Here is an educational enterprise which becomes more and more interfused with life's other meaningful activities.

> "Learners of different ages and stages would also be allowed to learn side by side, so that special kinds of inter-learning between generations would occur." [19]

At a conference in Washington, D.C. a short time ago, I shared the platform with Maggie Kuhn who heads up the Gray Panthers. Seventy-two years of age, at that time, and looking over her granny glasses at the audience, Maggie Kuhn spoke of the values of community colleges in reducing chasms between age groups. She decried age-segregated institutions that appear to be developing in our society. She looks upon young and old as natural partners; they need each other. And she suggested that a new kind of extended family could be set up in the learning community of the community college with lines going out into the surrounding area from that college setting. She spoke of the need for learning that could retool and renew for a new understanding of life, and of the advantages of education for new roles and responsibilities over the "playtime" concept of the retired years.

To Reduce Age Divisions

There may be serious generational conflicts in the United States unless ways are found to ease the dependency role of a rapidly-growing sector of our population and to reverse the age-segregation trend. Reference has been made previously to the Silver-Haired Legislature in Florida and its political power. Young people whose pay deductions for Social Security take an ever larger part of their pay checks could possibly see those contributions not so much as deposits toward their own retirement but rather as compulsory payments to support a growing leisure class. Self-interest of the producers could very well come into serious conflict with self-interest of persons who have been assigned by society, and sometimes by their own perceptions, to non-productive roles. As Maggie Kuhn has pointed out, educational institutions could help reduce the chasms.

A community college trustee comments in a letter along a similar vein:

> . . . there is a trend toward steering older people away from the mainstream of whatever is going on when in fact they should be brought more directly into the mainstream. Rather than putting them out to pasture, we should bring them into the classroom in all areas. They will benefit intellectually and the younger students will benefit as well . . . If we are taking courses into factories where people

work, are we also taking them into housing for the elderly where people are retired? If we are actively recruiting high school graduates are we also actively recruiting persons who may not have been in high school for forty years?

If we develop courses for women entering the world of work, do we develop courses for people leaving the world of work? If we develop courses for people beginning their married life and child rearing, do we develop courses for older people facing widowhood or the need to cope with serious prolonged illness?

Changes are taking place. Art Buchwald noted something that struck him as quite different when he gave a commencement address at a community college. Usually the proud parents are in the audience and applaud as their sons and daughters walk across the stage to receive their diplomas. At this institution, he reported, the sons and daughters and grandchildren were in the audience and they cheered as their parents and grandparents got the diploma and the president's handshake.

Need to Motivate

Special efforts are required if education is to truly span the generations. Patricia Cross reports that research data reveal the socialized perception that learning is for young people. "The feeling of being too old to learn increases steadily with age until it becomes a common barrier to education for older people." [20] On the other hand, the age factor is more likely to be perceived as a barrier by those who have never participated in continuing education than by those who have. If participation by older people in learning activities is judged to be a matter of societal importance as well as individual benefit, educational institutions can find ways to greatly increase the numbers of older learners. They have done that with minorities, athletes, bright students, women, and refugees. The major barriers, reports Dr. Cross, to group participation of the elderly are motivational in the sense that many contend that they are too old, lack energy, or are not interested in further education. Location is also a serious problem for the elderly.

Motivations are susceptible to change. In Sweden, studies showed, as they have elsewhere, that the people participating in adult learning activities are primarily "the already relatively well-educated young ones." [21] Since the middle of the 1960's there has been discussion about how to achieve a better balance in the nation between education among adults and young people. National policies were adopted to lessen what was described as an existing gap in education between the generations. Up to ten years ago, adult education was addressed primarily to people who took the intiative in demanding educational opportunities. Then it was recognized that more active recruitment methods were required to awaken an interest in education among certain categories of adults. The largest target group consisted of older people with six or seven years of primary schooling who had never enrolled for any further education. Their needs were addressed through study circle programs, sometimes in combination with courses organized by folk high schools, municipal and national adult schools, educational broadcasts combined with correspondence courses or study circles, or in conjunction with labor market training and trade union courses. It was discovered that the strong commitment to adult education tended to widen the educational and training gaps between people rather than to narrow them.

Now new efforts toward outreach are being extended and collaboration encouraged among agencies and organizations in adult education. "Outreaching" activities show favorable results. During the three years 1975-1978, 10 educational associations participated in such projects in housing areas. More than 1300 callers listened to and talked with 130,000 persons about their rights and possibilities in adult education. As a result, about 20,000 of them began educational work. The main purpose of the activity was to inform people with low basic education about their rights and possibilities of study. Recruitment was a subsequent matter. Experimentation has led to the conclusion that outreaching activity should be a natural and permanent element in adult education. The Swedish experiment is in line with the conclusions of Cross that "lack of information becomes the new barrier, operating to exclude those who might stand to benefit most from new kinds of learning opportunities." [22]

There is good reason to believe that an effective means of providing information is through existing networks of organizations in which the persons to be contacted are already involved.

Family Study Cuts Across Age

Tremendous stress experienced by another social institution provides unparalleled opportunities to bring together "learners of different ages and stages." Urgency of family problems is increasing nationwide. Recent reports indicate that nearly all of our entire human service system is remedial, rather than preventative, and that it advocates preventative methods of handling family crises in order to reduce the need for expensive remedial help. For San Francisco Community College District this is not a new matter. Over the past 20 years, programs have been offered to help people understand their responsibilities as parents, their children's needs, and have provided valuable instruction in parenting skills. A recent report lists the following programs:

Preparation for Childbirth (Lamaze)
Parent Participation Preschools
Parents of School Age Children
Parent in the Business Community
Family Daycare Training
Parents of Children in Foster Placement
Parent/Child Development for Incarcerated Women

Parent/Infant Development
Parent/Child Development
State Preschool Project
Effective Parenting/Adolescent Development
Single Parenting
Foster Parent Training
Campus Child Development Center

''Parenting is the most difficult and least valued occupation,'' according to the program director at the San Francisco college. Further:

> Training in parenting skills is desperately needed because of changing sociological factors such as the increased numbers of women who are divorced, working or single parents or those who are parenting in a blended family situation. With these new family situations, parents have requested help in understanding developmental processes, so realistic expectations of child behavior can help them guide and assist their children to become productive members of society. With these understandings, the entire community benefits.[23]

In 1977-78, parent education programs in San Francisco served more than eight thousand students, and almost that number in 1978-79, even with a cut in budget. Many of the programs involve parents *and their children*. Classes often serve as significant support systems to new mothers or those who may be having difficulties with children.

The importance of the adolescent years is getting new attention. Urie Bronfenbrenner has described the importance of that period and the problem of age-segregation as it relates to that part of a person's life. In response to the question, "What age do you feel is most critical for the development of human potential?," he said:

> I was once asked the same question . . . at a Senate hearing. I knew I was expected to say the first six years, but I said the junior-high-school years instead. Nowadays they're the most critical in terms of the destructive effects on a young person's development . . . this youthful stage is just as critical as the earlier childhood stage. Both are entry points into the problems of people not caring. Right now, the junior-high-school is often a disintegrating, alienating world. You can get competent, able, compassionate kids coming into that system, and junior high can turn them into kids out of *Lord of the Flies*. Junior-high-school isn't just segregated from different ages, but from almost everything about society . . . junior high is one of the most isolated institutions we have, and that's dangerous. The main reason for the unsafe and increasingly vandalized culture of junior high is that there are . . . no challenges or real responsibilities. Lack of responsibility is a real problem. The inutility of childhood in America is a striking fact. We don't let our children do anything important. They're useless because we have made them useless. They have no experience in being responsible for other human beings.[24]

Staff of the parent education program say that, although the values of our culture are being blamed, "it is not impossible to begin to turn the situation around by increasing parents' awareness of the critical role they must play in helping the adolescent to arrive at a value system that is humanistic, caring, and responsible."

Obviously education of this kind is not effective if it is conceived as limited to the community college classroom and laboratory. There are great advantages and possibilities when the college is perceived to be part of a community network which surrounds the family: schools, recreation centers, health agencies, neighborhood organizations, employers, social agencies, and the myriad of other institutions that cut across age lines and influence individual and community development. The strongest kind of case can be made for the value of parent education programs. A most perplexing question is why that fact is not more obvious to those whose responsibility it is to organize such programs and to those who authorize the necessary support.

On second thought, that is not really the most perplexing question. One of even greater importance is that of—how we assess a need? Who assigns importance? Does a 50-year-old man need a course in ethics or philosophy? In ordering of priorities, would he rank higher or lower the young woman of 18 who "needs" a course in calculus, or a mother and father who seek learning for more effective "parenting?" How do we validate a need? On the basis of the individual's declaration or a judgment made by some other party or agency? Is a program to prepare for employment of greater need than one for the more creative utilization of leisure time? Are "credit" courses of greater worth and hence more representative of real needs than "non credit" courses? As we move more in the direction of inter-learning between the generations a different scale of values will be required.

"Learning and living, which have drifted apart, stand in need of 'reintegration.' The educational structures required to achieve this goal will involve learning not only throughout life, but in all aspects of life."[25]

Reintegration of learning and living will come as our view of the learners rises beyond the campus and its "students" to the people of the community, the potential learners—their problems, conditions, aspirations, possibilities, and resources. This does not represent a new direction for many community colleges. To provide an effective teaching-learning process for the remarkable diversity of human talent seeking its services, it is essential to know the communities in which the students live, to understand their rootage systems. People, students and teachers alike, move off campus and into the communities to gain that understanding. Relationships are forged involving health, housing, recreation, community action, family life, political movements, employment services, libraries, day-care centers, museums, labor unions, and churches. The colleges are changed by new clienteles, and an essential and significant change is that of the transition of an institution from a state of being set apart to a condition of meeting people where they are, spatially and educationally.

As has been indicated before, however, our terminology is not up-to-date and in line with our affirmations. We persist in applying somewhat denigrating terminology to a majority of the learners. They are called part-time students, a term which carries an implication that they are somewhat less worthy than full-time students—and the truth is that now, in terms of public financial support, they seem to be. The term insinuates that somewhere along the line they must have missed the boat. Similarly, "part-time" faculty conveys an inferior status. Such labels don't fit the mission.

Some of the most effective teaching will be done by "professor-practitioners." Having achieved competence in their profession, in industry, in their trades, in business, in government, in social organizations, they continue to practice and to teach. One possible result—less likelihood of "yesterday's personnel teaching on yesterday's equipment."

Bringing the Parts Together

Why does it seem so difficult to establish a working relationship with other organizations in the community that affect the quality of life and that contribute toward the development of human potential? A force as strong as gravity seems to operate to pull us back to home base and the warmth and security of "homefolks." Education does not stand alone in less developed countries. A "sector" approach is used which encompasses training and human resource development in related fields, such as agriculture, industry, health, nutrition, and public service. Education is perceived to have "multiple intersections with almost every facet of national development." Experience in developing societies may make it possible for us to see that one of institutionalized education's major mistakes has been to stay on campuses—educational enclaves distant from interaction of people in the cities, on the farms, in group life, family life, and government. The community college gives some evidence of turning that process around.

Alan Pifer, president of the Carnegie Corporation and a distinguished American leader, said in a keynote address to the fifty-fourth annual convention of the American Association of Community and Junior Colleges in February 1973:

Other institutions will have a part to play, of course, but I see the community college as the essential leadership agency. Indeed, I'm going to make the outrageous suggestion that community colleges should start thinking about themselves from now on only secondarily as a sector of higher education and regard as their primary role community leadership . . . Not least, they can become the hub of a network of institutions and community agencies—the high schools, industry, the church, voluntary agencies, youth groups, even the prison system and the courts—utilizing their educational resources and, in turn, becoming a resource for them.

The focus is on people—people in the community. A cooperative effort in San Diego illustrates the essential orientation. In the heart of an economically depressed area, the community college district, in cooperation with city, county, and federal governments, has built an Educational Cultural Complex which provides vocational training, basic and academic education, career counseling, child development programs, a community theater, a food service facility, and other community-oriented functions. It is designed as an adult community center. The city of San Diego has built a branch of its public library system in the complex. The complex serves as a "one-stop" adult center for meeting the needs of the southeast San Diego community and its citizens in a creative, innovative way.[26]

Emphasis on People

Community colleges are sometimes called "People Colleges," and "Democracy's Colleges," and "Opportunity Colleges." Whatever the term used, they connote informality, accessibility, practical approaches, a cooperative stance, and high value placed on individual and community development. The point of beginning and continuing reference is the learning needs and interests of the people, not the syllabus, the book, the course, the professor, the institution. This outlook can integrate living and learning. A very simple set of statements can describe this point of view.

1. We look at people.
2. We see educational needs.
3. We seek to meet some of those needs.
4. We do not seek to meet all of those needs.
5. We are aware that other resources are available.
6. We seek to stimulate an awareness in learners of all of the resources.
7. We work with other resource providers in identification of needs.
8. We work with other providers in making resources visible and attainable.
9. We observe that human development is lifelong.
10. Human development involves learning.
11. Learning which is lifelong can benefit from education.
12. The community—a collective of individuals—also will benefit.

Our aim is to develop a community of learners. The qualities sought are independence, self-reliance, and cooperation, not a condition of dependency upon an educational monopoly. The outlook proposed is optimistic. It speaks of resources, awareness, learning, human development, and the benefit of education. Learning is perceived as an essential element in living. Community colleges are a lively development—an educational movement that has evolved remarkable potential to take us through to the next era of education—from adult education to lifelong education. But the "movement" requires careful handling. The life can be squeezed out of it. Not that the lifelong learning surge will be defeated. It will prevail, in time. But whether community colleges will have a big piece of the action and whether they will exercise their potential toward accelerating developments, that is the question. Will community colleges continue in sensitive and perceptive ways to shape themselves to meet emerging individual and community needs? It is that stance which has brought no little success to date and only that stance which guarantees a future.

The critical question, then, facing policy makers and educational leaders is—*What part does the community college play in the learning society of the '80's?*

[1] Paul Lengrand. *An Introduction to Lifelong Education*. Paris: UNESCO, 1970, p. 44.

[2] Edgar Faure et al. *Learning to Be: The World of Education Today and Tomorrow*. Paris: UNESCO, 1972.

[3] R. H. Dave. *Foundations of Lifelong Education*. Paris: UNESCO, 1976.

[4] Ibid. p. 201.

[5] Carnegie Council on Policy Studies in Higher Education. *Giving Youth a Better Chance*. San Francisco: Jossey-Bass, 1979, p. 22.

[6] Ibid. p. 25.

[7] Gail Sheehy. *Passages*. New York: Bantam Books, 1977.

[8] Vivian R. McCoy. *Lifelong Learning: The Adult Years*. Washington, D.C.: Adult Education Association of the U.S.A., October 1977.

[9] R. H. Dave. Op. cit. p. 360.

[10] Ibid. p. 209.

[11] Leonard Woodcock. "Education for a New Age: A Partnership With Labor." *Community and Junior College Journal* 45: 15-20; May 1975.

[12] Samuel C. Brightman. *Newsletter*, National Council of Senior Citizens, 1977.

[13] "Working Paper, Meeting of Experts on the Content of Education in the Context of Life-Long Learning." Paris, September 8, 1975. (Translated from French.)

[14] College Entrance Examination Board. *Career Transition: The Demand for Counseling, Volume I*. New York: the Board, 1977

[15] New York State Education Department, Division of Continuing Education. "New York State Continuing Education Needs Assessment. Report No. 1: Statewide Analysis." Albany: the Department, 1977

[16] Howard Bowen. "A Nation of Educated People." *Community and Junior College Journal* 49: 6-14, May 1979

[17] Dorothy M. Knoell. *Through the Open Door. A Study of Patterns of Enrollment and Performance in California's Community Colleges*. Report No. 76-1. Sacramento: California Postsecondary Education Commission, February 1976.

[18] Ibid.

[19] R. H. Dave. Op. cit. p. 350.

[20] Richard E. Peterson and Associates. *Lifelong Learning in America*. San Francisco: Jossey-Bass, 1979, pp. 75 ff.

[21] Osten Groth. Unpublished report, Tarendo, Sweden, 1979.

[22] K. Patricia Cross. "Community College Students Today and Tomorrow." Address given to the Arizona Community College Board, Phoenix, Arizona, February 16, 1979.

[23] Rosemary Darden. "Parent Education Program." Unpublished report, San Francisco Community College District, 1977.

[24] S. Byrne, editor. "Nobody Home: The Erosion of the American Family." A Conversation with Urie Bronfenbrenner. *Psychology Today* 10: 40-43; May 1977.

[25] R. H. Dave. Op. cit. p. 348.

[26] Dale Parnell. "Needed: An Urban Extension Act." *Community and Junior College Journal* 49: 10-13; October 1978.

[27] Ibid. p. 12.

Chapter V

LEGISLATIVE PERCEPTIONS

I n these pages I have been sketching a picture of the possibilities and promise of the community college. Put in general terms, as such statements need to be, I envision its mission to encourage and facilitate lifelong learning with community as process and product. In doing that, one of its primary functions is to aid those in the community who want to learn how to secure certain basic necessities. Among these: housing, health, employment, food, and citizenship rights and responsibilities. And it needs to do more than that—to be creatively occupied with the community, perform a vital function in an integrated system of community services. Instillation of a true sense of community is the aim, a condition where people can learn to communicate, where there can be a sense of connection and interchange of thoughts and ideas.

The community colleges reveal traits that forecast a crucial role in the establishment of American education upon such concepts as the following:

1. An educational organization in which all citizens have access to education at a time when they feel the need of such

access, and under circumstances in which they find the experience congenial and stimulating.

2. Adults are capable of learning throughout life and it is increasingly important that they actually do so.

3. Learners of different ages and stages should be allowed to learn side by side so that special kinds of inter-learning between generations can occur.

4. Learning and living, which have drifted apart, stand in need of "reintegration." The educational structures required to achieve this goal will involve learning not only throughout life, but in all aspects of life.

To what extent does the broad stroke picture described above depict existing educational policy as well as current perceptions and goals of legislators and state level officials? Frank conversations with public officials in several states lead to the impression that substantial differences exist between the views proposed and the current state of legislative perceptions and policies.

What Is the State Interest?

Why should we be concerned to any great extent about legislative attitudes and the views of state-level officials if the community college destiny is so interwoven with the local scene? The answer to that question can be found in developments over the past 10 years that reveal the strong hand of "economic determinism." The effect has been to shift, in large part, the determination of the fortunes of this institution from the local to the state level. A state official in California described that process as he saw it unfold there. In general, what he reports holds true for many other states. Here is the gist of what he said.

The traditional expectation of the community college role in California was to provide open access to students moving into higher education systems. One of the significant policy statements with regard to the community colleges was found in the master plan adopted in 1960. Little was indicated then about the role of the institutions other than that they should be open door and related in their functions to the University of California, the California state universities and colleges, and the private institutions.

The next major policy stage was brought into being in the late 1960's through the act which established the Board of Governors of the California community colleges. Tied to it was the issue of local control. At that time, the state was contributing only about 35-40 percent of the funding for operations, the rest came from local taxes, the generation of which was the responsibility of local boards. In effect, through the late '60's and early '70's the community colleges were benignly neglected by the state, left free to pursue whatever course they chose.

The institutions then entered a period of rapid expansion in the early 1970's. They became involved in many new areas of activity—the reentry of women, programs for older persons, and applied vocational programs without participation or interference from the state capital. There were two events, however, that eventually brought these institutions into sharp focus in Sacramento. The first had to do with adult education. It was not until about May, 1973, that people at the state level saw the big jump in ADA (average daily attendance, the factor upon which state financing is based) which resulted to a great extent from the growing move of community colleges into the adult field. Some high government officals were critical of some of the courses that were being taught. A limit was placed on enrollment of retired people and an attempt was made to avoid fiscal incentives which would encourage further developments of this kind.

By this time about 45 percent of funding was provided by the state, though local control pertained. The Commission on Postsecondary Education was charged to study the financing of these institutions. Then Proposition 13 hit and totally changed the picture. As local taxes were reduced, state funds were required to maintain community colleges. Currently, about 70 percent of the budget comes from the state and there are more state general fund dollars going to community colleges than go to the University of California or to the state university system. The community colleges are now the "major fund grabbers."

Yet, the president of the University of California bewails the fact that the university is losing its prestige as related to Harvard and Yale and the University of Michigan. And when he talks about the university, he is not talking only about Berkeley and UCLA. He's talking about the entire university system; he wants it to equal those other institutions.

So the state has reached a point where it has to have a say and it has to ask: What are community colleges? And what are they doing?

The state needs to draw some lines. We have to ask what the state priorities are in funding community colleges.

A member of the Board of Governors of the California Community Colleges shared his insights into the process of community college evolution. It was his impression that the genius of these institutions has been in their adaptive qualities, often without deliberate planning. He described them as being in their adaptation like organisms in the forest. Community colleges have moved into areas of interest to various publics. The question is, then, should the state ratify these kinds of moves? They are cost-associated, thus are of major concern as governments attempt to control costs. What form of adaptation—what form of growth—will be supported or not supported? Until recently, the colleges could take the people who wanted to come. Now the legislature is asking—who are these people? Although there is tremendous support for the institutions, community colleges by and large are not understood by the legislators. The solons are more familiar with the four-year colleges.

The persisting issue appears to be—"should the state ratify these moves?"

State Government Also Changes

We miss something very important in our study of community colleges, however, if we assume that while these institutions are evolving state government remains unchanged. The fact is that state government has its own adaptive experiences to parallel those of the college. In a midwestern state, an astute observer who was identified with community colleges described it somewhat like this:

> Now we are driven to a great extent by legislative attitudes toward us. The legislative staff is greatly expanded. In the 1960's the legislature made biennial appropriations, but with the new constitution in 1970, they moved toward annual appropriations and, in effect, now there is a full-time legislature. Their salaries have been increased. Now the governor can veto on line items or can veto reductions. Formerly, it was either veto or not veto. You are halfway through the funding year, sometimes, before you know what the appropriation process is going to hold for you. Staff in the legislature has grown enormously. This was not the case 10 or 15 years ago. There has been a great change in the politics of this state. There are professional lobbyists from many groups with their power resting to some extent on the information that they have at hand.

The legislative staff are characteristically analytical. They are accustomed to computer use and they talk in terms of cost-effective systems. They are intent upon assisting the legislators to satisfy vast hordes of people, to try to make these legislators look good by cutting appropriations. Now, too, there is a bureau of the budget in the House and the Senate which has its own budget people. And there is a budget officer for the executive with hard-nosed analysts staffing the office.

On the other hand, they have a community college board staff of about 30 people and they are really not able to compete. The community colleges are not capable of doing it. There is not a good research function in the state available to community colleges or in the institutions. They cannot relate well to the state staff, so in effect, then, the state staff are becoming the philosophers indicating the way to go. And unless we do something like those who originally put the system together, we will not move. Question is, where can we find those entrepreneurs?

As some unknown pundit has put it, where you stand depends upon where you sit. One fact is clear; two changing social institutions, state government and community colleges, each having its own perceptions of accountability, are becoming increasingly interactive.

Supportive and Inquiring Attitudes

How do legislators and state officials feel about community college change? What are they concerned about? How do they view what is happening?

By and large they are supportive of the institutions. And although a few years ago it might have been necessary to have told them what I meant by community colleges, that is no longer necessary. Legislators have mixed views of what they are and should be, but they are well aware of their existence. Said one of the senior legislators, chairman of a powerful committee, "Community colleges offer damn good education at that level. I'm very supportive. If you wanted negative comments, you came to the wrong man." His opinion might have been influenced by his daughter's successful experiences in a community college. Other key legislators hold that the state is getting its money's worth and that the colleges "do an extraordinary job of adjusting to community needs." However, it is the question of how "adjustable" they should be that is much on the minds of the policy makers. These are the comments you hear. They have a common theme—that it is time to examine community college mission:

> Can we continue to fund at an adequate level community colleges that have taken on such awesome responsibilities?

> This state, like California, has just turned the corner on funding issues for education. State aid for community colleges will need to go to 58 percent. Time was never more ready for an examination of mission.

> There is a need for extensive hearings on this whole issue to explore the state's interest in adult education. There may be some pulling back or withdrawing. There will be more emphasis upon meeting the economic needs of society and preparing employment skills—more emphasis upon academic education as a means toward continuing education.

> The community colleges represent a good system. The state is getting good value, but at the same time we will be engaged in the process of tightening things up.

As we shall see, the remarkable growth of community colleges and consequent need for public funds; the proportionate increase in funding from the state level stemming from citizen antipathy to mounting property taxes; limitation measures on state budgets; the mounting costs of other social programs; the impact of inflation; and the changing demographic scene, are among the factors that cause legislators to assert: "The state has reached a point where it has to have a say and to ask—what are community colleges and actually what are they doing?"

Austerity for the Public Sector

Talk with legislators about the future of education and very soon the conversation is about money and the taxpayer's mood and responsibilities. Not only does inflation make it difficult to maintain the status quo, but available funds have been limited by Proposition 13 in California and similar tax cutting measures in other states. Some describe this as an age of austerity for the public sector in which the emphasis is on what we can afford to spend rather than on what our educational needs may be. Some taxpayers, they observe, feel that we've already gone too far, that we have been serving wants rather than needs, that it is the private sector which should serve wants.

What can we afford is a common refrain. "With tight resources, increasing questions are being raised as to whether we can afford to implement that ideal—every American has the right to education." The legislator might feel that community college and adult and continuing education should be expanded but "taxpayers will ask if it is worthwhile." And how do you make a cost benefit case along those lines? What is it worth for a person to have some sense of satisfaction?

In some states community colleges began their big growth simultaneous with the adoption of such measures as income taxes. A vast amount of money was available, say some of the interviewees, and new developments included not only community colleges but programs in mental health and other social fields. In the late 1960's, "things really boomed." Now the bonanza is used up, was one report, and "if the true picture were known the state is in the red and the county I am from is going bankrupt." So how do we prioritize the state's limited resources? Said one observer:

> In the forefront of our attention as a result of court decisions will be problems in the fields of mental health and correctional facilities. We're going to have to give some attention to those areas. Corrections and mental health have moved up in priority and as we look at what might happen to the automotive industry with changes there and possible high unemployment, the social service area might very well be open-ended. So education, period, is not the highest priority.

Some legislators are deeply concerned about public attitudes toward education and its support. They wonder how taxpayers feel about paying for "remediation" for students who have already had and failed their opportunities in the schools at taxpayers' expense. They wonder whether the education community is as prudent with expenditures as it could be.

"What will it cost," appears to be a significant question in the shaping of educational policy. For example, some legislative staff were of the opinion that vocational-technical programs as well as adult education might well be provided by the public schools rather than community colleges as a means of cutting state costs. On the other hand, legislators several times proposed expanding the university-parallel or transfer programs because the costs, as they saw it, would be less for the taxpayer and the student if students began their post high school educations in the community college.

State legislators seem to be interested in the effect of community college services on the state's financial commitments, "the state's interest," as it is usually put. It was indicated often that the college could do whatever it wanted with local resources. There is somewhat of a dilemma here, of course, inasmuch as the trend is toward a proportionate decline in resources at the local level, and hence a shrinking of local determination.

On the other hand, community college personnel might take heart at the admissions of the members of a county legislature: "The faculty and the students and the administrators have to realize that we don't live, breathe, and sleep education. We've got other things to think about and to do."

State-level policy makers and agency heads are thinking about education *and* "other things." A major factor in decision making will be that of the ordering of priorities in terms of financial resources that apparently have little prospect for growth. Legislative concerns include the necessity for consolidation and reallocation. Cost factors figure prominently in the decision making process. In fact, at this time, nothing seems to preoccupy legislators more than do financial matters. A college official noted:

> The tax limitation proposal did pass here and this establishes parameters of growth. We'll have to work with these. We'll have to fight to hold what we have. It's hard to do that when the overall picture is one of decline.

Winding Down the Apparatus

Legislators, their staffs, and the agency personnel have looked with alarm at the charts and the graphs which show the declining numbers of youth coming out of the schools over the next decade and more. In one state, an official in the governor's office reported that in elementary education 50,000-60,000 people are being lost annually. The decline is among people who would be served by the schools and later by colleges and universities. Hence the inevitable result: a winding down of the educational apparatus at all levels. Consequently, appropriation authorities expect that financial requirements will not be as great. The aid formula which has been commonly adopted by legislators is enrollment-driven—the more sutdents the larger the financial requirements. Logically, the reverse is perceived also to apply—the fewer students the smaller the financial requirements. Attempts to try to change the argument now, in the opinion of that state-level official, will fall on deaf ears: "There is a real potential for loss of priority for education in this state. The enrollment factor has been the key.''

At the time of this examination, enrollments in some post-secondary institutions had already dropped, though the last of the big classes out of the senior high schools are only now being graduated. In one state, for example, a state university built to accommodate 20,000 students had dropped from 22,000 to 13,500. Obviously, according to a state official, the institution encountered serious problems in its programming. The school is still maintaining as its major emphasis the social sciences and education. It has not geared up for change. Legislators considered community colleges to be in a stronger position than four-year institutions in the face of declining enrollments.

''Why shouldn't there be a decline in the number of people going to community colleges since public school enrollments are going down?'' In a southern state that question was put by staff of House and Senate committees on education. I asked whether state planning was taking into account frequent career shifts of the adult population as well as the growing number of women entering post-secondary institutions to qualify for meaningful employment. I referred to the large number of people in their late forties or early fifties retiring from such fields as the automotive industry who wanted to work, who found it necessary to supplement retirement benefits, and who consequently needed new job skills. I pointed to the increased population of older people with keen interests in learning activities who may not have had time, nor opportunity, for such pursuits earlier in their lives. The reply: ''You've got some good points there.''

To summarize, policy makers and their staffs are directing their attention largely to declining numbers of school-age children and the implications thereof for college and university enrollments. Generally, their perceptions are of children moving up through the schools into colleges and ''out to life.'' The view is seldom broad enough to register the effect and the meaning of that population wave that has been passing through our institutions for the past 15 years or so *and continues to carry active educational needs and interests*.

Viewed in Traditional Terms

Education is something for the young. That viewpoint still appears to be dominant among state policy makers. Enrollees in community colleges are generally perceived to be 18 and 19 year-old youth. "You need to keep reminding them that the average age is now beyond 27," said a legislative staff member.

Not long ago the new Downtown Center of San Francisco Community College District was dedicated. The facilities are designed to serve some 10,000 students who are represented primarily in the thousands of people who work every day in that city. The mayor of San Francisco, speaking at the televised dedication ceremonies, congratulated the city on having such a fine new facility for "the youngsters." The fact is that many of those "youngsters" are in their forties, fifties, and beyond.

Moreover, the notion that it is the young who are primarily involved in education continues to condition federal as well as state legislation. Testifying before the United States Senate Committee on Labor and Human Resources on "Alternative Missions for Higher Education in the 80's," I tried to dispel the erroneous assumption—upon which much of the Higher Education Act is based—that higher education serves mainly 18 to 22-year-old, full-time students, enrolled in liberal arts programs. The data show that only 51 percent of the postsecondary enrollments in the entire country are 18 to 24-year old dependents.

There are exceptions to the above generalizations. A prominent state senator, a former Fulbright scholar, speaks of the 29 community colleges in his state as a blessing to the state and to the communities.

> They have served functions attracting the non-traditional students, the housewives, the veterans, the dropouts. They provide a more supportive service, in my estimation, than other institutions, and particularly are appealing to senior citizens and to those who had not recognized the value of education when they were younger.

There are three areas of community college programming upon which a strong consensus exists: occupational, transfer, and remediation. Everybody seems to be completely in favor of occupational education. From trustee to state legislator, this would seem to be favored as one of the essential programs of community colleges. Nationally, the enrollments in this field now surpass those in the transfer programs, which are also seen as important for community colleges to continue, particularly for those who otherwise would not have access to the college opportunity. Legislators often appear surprised at the large proportion of persons involved in occupational programs. A county legislature, for example, had been under the impression that the focus of the college program was on liberal arts, which they saw as less than desirable because of the existence of other college programs in their area. When they found out that 70 percent of the students were in career programs and 30 percent in the liberal arts, they were amazed—and they approved. Perhaps this situation tells us something about the need for better communication. The legislators said there had been "a real hassle" on the budget during their last session, yet, had they known the institution was so heavily oriented toward the occupational fields, their views might have been changed. They felt that the percentage of occupational programs as related to the liberal arts was satisfactory.

In general, strong support continues for college-transfer programs. In fact, it was suggested frequently that these should be strengthened. The current interest in all of higher education in career-oriented programs may have the effect of increasing community college enrollments in lower-division courses. A number of universities, it was reported to me, are finding it necessary to limit the number of students in such popular fields as science, computer applications, business management, engineering, health technologies, public service administration, and mechanical engineering technology. Consequently, more students begin such programs in community colleges.

The university-parallel, transfer programs, are not impervious to the scrutiny of legislators. Some questions are being asked about their quality. In one state it was pointed out that when the community college system was launched in 1957 that the central thrust in planning was "access." Now, it was stated, assessment is a major concern, particularly in relation to how well students are prepared to transfer to four-year colleges and universities. In that state, questions of competence were under consideration with respect to both the entry and exit of community college students. Should high school completers who had not scored well on the public school minimal competency tests be eligible for admission to community colleges? And should there be a similar instrument developed for use in the community colleges before the associate degree is conferred? Needless to say there were mixed opinions on both questions, and, it is fair to say, the integrity of the grading system in the community colleges was under question by the commissioner of education and legislators. There is unmistakable concern about the need to improve literacy at all levels—in the schools, the community colleges, and the universities.

If people are not functionally literate upon leaving institutions where presumably they were to learn those skills, there is a body of opinion that says they stand in need of remediation. It is possible to find that word only in the most recently published dictionaries, though it is currently in wide use. The word is related to the verb and noun "remedy," which includes such meanings as, "Any medicine or application which puts an end to disease and restores health;" "also one that relieves, but does not necessarily end, a morbid condition;" "That which corrects or counteracts an evil; a corrective, cure." In law, it is the legal means to recover a right, or to prevent, or obtain redress for a wrong. Other meanings include: to cure; relieve; correct; repair. All of these trigger thoughts about why students cannot read and write and add and subtract.

Many say corrective measures are needed. Others say the person has a *right* to minimum competency. Regardless of whose fault it might be, large numbers of people leave the elementary and secondary schools not having reached desired minimum levels of performance in reading (or language arts) and mathematics. Call it remediation or developmental education, state legislators and agency heads consider the educational need represented to be an appropriate one for community college response. There is no great enthusiasm noted about such programs, but the necessity is acknowledged, perhaps reluctantly, with the hope expressed that in time the problem will be rectified in the earlier years of education. It is commonly perceived that remediation should not be the job of higher education, but as long as the elementary and secondary institutions are not doing it, then the community colleges should.

Legislators wonder, though, how long you can justify to the taxpayers the costs associated with such services, as one observed:

> Remedial programs in the community college are worthwhile. It's something they have to do, but it is difficult to justify that to the public when it comes to matters of appropriations. They have already made their resources available so people could learn these skills in the elementary and secondary schools. Why should it have to be done again at the college level? How much should you really do for a person?

One of the most thoughtful comments about this problem in our society came from a faculty member rather than a legislator and needs to be heard by all policy shapers in the educational field. She was of the opinion that students in the K–12 years had not been taught to learn. As we discussed the implications of that fact for lifelong education, she pointed out how the gap will continue to widen between the "haves and have-nots" in education if people in those early years are not taught how to learn. The early deficiencies tend to be cumulative in effect, like barnacles on the bottom of a boat.

Beyond these three programs, occupational, university-parallel, and remediation, views of legislators tend to scatter, especially in relation to funding possibilities. Undoubtedly there will be more adult education and not as much attention to credit, said one official, but it will be difficult for some people to appreciate this for purposes of funding. "I have no difficulty with the open access pipeline to community colleges," said another, "with job-related programs, certificated programs, and upgrading of job skills, but beyond that it becomes a very political matter."

Recreational-type programs, arts and crafts, and "developing the facility to get along in society," were described as worthwhile activities but "this field remains an issue in the state." Other similar comments were heard:

> The Governor and the Legislature want to protect the integrity of the core courses of the general programs and the academic. They have a strong position on this.

> If somehow or another there was a basic skills component or a job-related component then there wouldn't be any question about it. It would be considered appropriate.

An influential official in California voiced the sentiments of a good many legislators. He did not mind that only 50,000 out of more than one million community college students in California transferred to the universities so long as the work in those institutions could be described as academic and upgrading, appropriate to something that is called a college. For him, that concept has been softened at the edges by the inclusion of various kinds of social services. "Perhaps we should call it a community activities center," he said, "or redefine what we mean by a college."

Concern About the "Soft" Areas

Two questions are much debated in the states as the mission of community colleges is given new and searching attention. What are the truly legitimate services which institutions should provide? And who should pay for the services? Legislators tend to refer to some services as "soft," or "leisure," or "luxury." An analysis of responses yields a number of clues to what are considered to be soft areas. Among them are education for human fulfillment, social services, expansion of self, personal fulfillment, keeping people busy in old folks' homes, self actualization, adult and continuing services, recreational, avocational and hobby-type courses, leisure time programs, and non-degree oriented activities. A sampling of comments reveals some rather definite opinions:

> I don't believe community colleges have the responsibility of keeping people busy in old folks' homes. This isn't really their role to get in the field of social services and counseling in the community . . . you are getting into an area that's very, very soft.

> Programs offered in geriatric homes make people happy, no question about it, but I don't see the state's benefit. Perhaps these ought to be provided by people in rehabilitation or perhaps the people in the homes ought to be doing it themselves.

> I have no problem with services to that older client group and serving productive citizens who can contribute to the economy of the states. One of our problems is with the avocational, not with the person who is having a career change, but does the taxpayer owe to the Social Security recipients X number of dollars in order to provide recreational, avocational or hobby-type educational experiences? How do we prioritize the state's limited resources?

> There's a tough line to draw with respect to these (luxury) courses. What is really legitimate? What about dog grooming? Some people make this their livelihood, others do it for a hobby. There are some good arguments for senior citizens being happier people when they get older if they are involved in educational programs—people who are reaching out and trying to learn. This probably could be described as cost-effective.

In the views expressed above there are hints of the overriding concern of state legislators. It is the suitable role of the state that interests them, not so much the "legitimacy" of the educational services, or whether it is appropriate for the college to engage in certain activities. References to the "state's benefit," and the "state's limited resources" should be noted in the above statements. As one legislator puts it, "I think the community college should be in leisure programs but the issue is should the state's mission include these kinds of programs." Others say that the college can be all things to all people if it has the resources. The central issue is not whether they have the programs but whether state money is to be utilized. As mentioned previously, it is often said that the community colleges can do what they want with local resources. "It's okay if they can lobby the board of supervisors and get local support, but not state funds."

Although that seems to be the prevailing position, that someone, other than the state, should pay for the "soft" areas, the issue is far from being decided. In one state where funding was removed a few years ago several key legislators are calling for a review of the situation:

> As we look ahead, needs will surface that we are not now aware of. Age in these institutions will undoubtedly continue to climb, with emphasis upon part-time enrollments. It does not bother me to have leisure-time activities funded. Community-based education is very productive. Older citizens are recharging skills. They may be working on things that deal with the maintenance of their homes. Most importantly, we are plowing citizens back into the educational process that they might have thought was terminated. The state is better off as a result of this and we should not turn our backs on a funding mechanism for that kind of service. We need to look back at the total picture of social need.

The man speaking was chairman of the state senate finance committee.

In several states the emotional level of discussion about "soft" areas has been lowered by working out specific descriptions of the various kinds of educational programs—a taxonomy—along with indications of the sources of support. Usually it is beneficial to have some assurance that all parties to an issue have a somewhat similar picture of the problem under consideration. A budget officer was participating in hearings where "community education" was the subject of several spirited and adversarial presentations. He asked for a description of "community education" which might turn the considerations into more productive channels. Unfortunately, the chief protagonists had difficulty in making explicit what they were talking about. This brings to mind statements by high ranking, politically sophisticated officials in two of the states visited. After all the discussion about problems of funding, declining enrollments, "soft areas," and community college aspirations, their comments were:

> Community colleges need to stand up to the states and say, 'Here is our role,' and then do it well.

The institutions ought to try to develop their own mission and then make the case for resource needs around that mission rather than leaving this to the State Capitol . . . The community colleges should take the lead . . . they should work out their own approaches.

Change in institutions, college or government, does not usually come about quickly or easily. Legislators were sold on the technical education and transfer roles of community colleges. Now that new areas are under development their appropriateness is sure to be questioned. Legislators are concerned about off-campus work. They were sold on the need for campuses, and large appropriations for buildings. Today we speak in terms of convenience, as well as access, and of community-based programs. To change will require justification. And areas will be considered ''soft'' until their social utility is established. The case will have to be made.

Competition

Competition may appeal to legislators on the gridiron or in the free enterprise system, but it is a different matter in state-supported education. They see more intense competition for future dollars and by and large they don't like it. Three factors are heating up the atmosphere. More institutions show an interest in the adult learner; funding formulas are usually enrollment-driven; financial support of education is moving to the state level.

Adult education is an area of major concern:

In some counties the adult educators and the community colleges fight; in others there are agreements that exist.

We have dual and sometimes competing delivery systems, that is, with the community schools and the adult schools. I'm concerned about how these educational services can relate and about the ambitions of the people who direct these programs.

Competition is becoming fierce between the schools and the community colleges. We might just cut down on both sectors. There are some real turf protection tendencies among educators and competitiveness which is not healthy. In adult education we have the K–12, community colleges, and intermediate districts. Three areas all competing for state dollars.

In one state it was the hope of legislative staff that a rational and cost-effective approach could be made to division of labor. They said that the new governor wanted the state to assess needs in various areas, calculate what the costs would be for the state to have services provided to an indicated number of people, and determine which agency could do the job most effectively. At this point a suitable organization would be designated.

In another state, a bill had been introduced which emphasized the need for coordination. In this case, the institutions were to be related in a program toward full employment. Included were CETA prime sponsors, K–12, community colleges, and four-year institutions.

Concerns are expressed that competition among educational sectors will reduce public support of education. The president of the State Board of Education in California is convinced that the next two or three years are going to be a crucial period for public education in that state and he urges a coalition of all educational groups. "This is no time for a civil war. There is need for coalescence." He conceded that in the past the community colleges and the adult schools have "run into each other to some extent," but pleads for a "settling down" period. He believes "this is a matter in transition and it's going to go to local options."

In another state, the state superintendent of public instruction proposed unofficially that community colleges provide adult extended services for the population 18 and beyond. "You would have to do a hell of a job politically to get that accomplished," one legislator postulated. And one of his colleagues said that community colleges should be responsible for adult education. He described adult education as pretty well mixed up now with the schools in it, the community colleges and, increasingly, the universities. However, he expressed somewhat less concern than others. "This doesn't shake me up. I don't feel it's absolutely necessary to have all these things neat and tidy."

His was a minority viewpoint. Most state officials interviewed wanted less competition and more coordination in adult education. Another area over which there is slightly less tension is that of vocational education.

> There are Regional Occupational Programs and Centers. These institutions have capital funds. They provide training in printing and shops, TV repair, etc. Then there are other CETA programs, skills centers, high schools, community colleges—at least four different types of agencies in this training field. The question is, who should be doing these things? What makes sense?

There are vocational-technical institutions that are just a block away from community colleges and may be duplicative in their programs and with little or no relationship established. The local council is supposed to deal with this but this is not always happening.

Methods of calculating financial suport are blamed by legislators for contention among educational institutions. "The funding formulas are based on warm bodies," hence there is incentive to recruit any and all. At the same time that there is acknowledgement of the advisability of seeking other funding methods, there is a strong view that educators need to relate their efforts and work out a *modus operandi*. The Greeks, too, had a word for the desired condition—*Ataraxy*—"capable of coexisting in harmony." Here's a comment from a legislator:

> Maybe we need to have another funding source or method. But most importantly, they need to relate their efforts and work these things out themselves. We do not have time or the training for it and neither do the tax people. There is more of a leadership role required of educators. They can't expect the legislature to do this and they don't want the bureaucracy to come in and tell them what to do, but that's what will happen.

What is happening is that institutions which previously had not encountered each other at the same "watering hole" are now congregating at a common source of sustenance. For example, community colleges in California, prior to passage of Proposition 13, were not perceived as "competitors" by the colleges and universities of that state. At least, not to any great extent. Now, with two-thirds of their support coming from Sacramento, their relative position and, consequently, the way they are viewed by the university and the state university system, has changed.

We have already referred to other trend lines that result in a different order of institutional relationships. When public junior colleges concentrated on university-parallel programs they had little contact with the public schools, and there was little overlap in adult education. But in response to societal changes, the junior college became the comprehensive community college with adult education as its dominant function. Now the schools and community colleges are brought into a different kind of relationship even as the traditional constituents served by both kinds of institutions are declining in numbers.

Moreover, as long as vocational education was primarily secondary in nature and considered a minor program of community colleges, there were few confrontations with vocational schools. But in recent years social and economic influences have moved vocational education increasingly to postsecondary levels. Occupational education has become the major program in community colleges because of similar influences. Thus, vocational institutions supported through the school systems and community colleges are placed in new patterns of interaction which are potentially contentious.

What we are dealing with is the necessity for institutional adaptation to change. Change in the value of the dollar. Change in public views about taxes. Change in sources of tax funds, from property taxes to state general revenues. Change in demography, with fewer young people, greater numbers of older people. The trend lines tend to bring educational institutions into the same arena—yet the resources are limited. What promotes competition? Something limited in supply which is valued by each or all of the actors. Consequently, conditions have evolved which breed competition and conflict. New methods will be required to deal with these new circumstances. Present frustrations in part result from the persisting notion that somehow the old ways should continue to work.

Institutional Management

As the states' interests in community colleges mount with greater proportions of funding, they give increased attention to the management capabilities and the accountability efforts of local institutions. It was the view of a legislative analyst that community colleges' budgets are not as strictly reviewed as they would be at the state level, but they will be under severe pressures now to reconcile priorities and to either police themselves or, "we'll do it for them by the big stick approach." And he indicated that the "marginal activities" will be difficult to maintain. He said that people in the state capital are greatly·concerned about accountability at the local level and about the proficiency of management.

Another official echoed that opinion: "Some districts are well managed, but it's the view of the state capital that others are not well managed and the perception exists that the districts may not be open in their operations."

Although there is indication that legislators have questions about the management of some of the community colleges there are more frequent references to the need for "educational leadership" and "competent top management who can make a case for their institutions." And there is a definite view that, in working with governmental personnel at the state level, the community college representatives may not have their act put together.

Political Problems

Heard too often to be disregarded are reports from governmental personnel that community colleges draw more fire from legislators and staff than do other colleges and universities. It is alleged that they have "real problems in trying to communicate their roles at the state level." Nothing interested me more than to explore this perception because one would think the widespread network of institutions and the great numbers of people served would give them unmatched influence on political developments. What accounts for the apparent lack of sophistication in relating to the legislature? Among possible reasons are these:

> *Relative newness at the state level.* The community college is still the new kid on the block. The institutions have not developed a good system of relating to decision makers at the state level.

> There has not been an attempt to educate the policy makers as to what community colleges really are and what they have grown into. They are still perceived as institutions serving the 18-19 year old and engaged in basket weaving.

> Many people do not understand the mission of community colleges and have the suspicion that community college developments may be based less on philosophy than on desire for dollars.

> They are still relatively a new entity. As the public becomes better informed about them, they will not be viewed as second-class institutions.

> People don't see where they fit into the scheme of things.

> *Lack of a unified voice.* They need a spokesman. They need somebody out front. Apparently the presidents have been un-

able to agree on these things so that they could have a common front. There is no collective approach at the state level.

When people are talking to the legislature about matters of funding their institutions they need a unified voice.

One of the problems, of course, is that what is good for the community colleges of Chicago is not necessarily good for Lincoln Land Community College. The equalization factor in the formula sometimes is divisive.

Lack of reliable, accurate data. Legislators finally say, give us one set of data that is accurate and then we will talk about those things. The lawmakers lose patience. There has been improvement but there is still a long way to go and this is not to say that legislators are not supportive of these institutions.

The legislators cannot help but compare baccalaureate presidents and community college presidents. Baccalaureate presidents seem to have worked it out smoothly. They have their charts and they are suave. They make their presentations. Community colleges may not feel the need for that, but they need to refine and make more sophisticated their presentations. They need to do a job of proving, not just pleading.

They ought to be able to say to the legislature and to the governor, "Here are people who got jobs, here are people who are being trained." Why don't they do that? Several of the institutions do a fine job on that. Why can't they do it together? "They have failed to tell the governor and legislators what they are doing—to indicate what they are doing that really benefits the state."

As is the case with all studies and generalizations, these observations may not fit the specific situations in all locales. However, value can be derived from consideration and application of the comments where it is justified. Worth considering is the thought that the local orientation of community colleges and their appropriate stance of decision making at the local level may not automatically qualify their representatives to engage in collective effort in the state capital. It will take deliberate and well-conceived measures to maintain the values of both institutional self-determinism and collaborative activity. To what extent does the following statement by a legislator hold true?

> There will be more competition for future dollars. Community colleges will be the losers. They have less of a constituency and they do have local resources, but they have less of an alumni group. I really don't see them developing a lot of political power. They are less organized. They have too many heads. They are hybrid creatures. School districts, on the other hand, have been around for a long time. They know how to pull together. Community colleges are highly individualistic. Sometimes they are in competition with each other.

Looking at the Legislature

In the spirit of fair play, we need to turn the glass around now to learn how community college presidents view the legislature and other state officials. In the light of what has been reported it should come as no great surprise that the common theme is, "We are very much misunderstood." In fact, sometimes it is put more emphatically: "After all of our efforts, they don't know what the hell we are all about." The latter comment came, not in response to any question but was volunteered while a group of presidents discussed pending legislation. Some see the legislators as unappreciative of the broad diversity of programs. Others say that legislators believe the community college is trying to educate too many people, even "people who can't make it." Legislators perceive transfer programs as paramount. They complain about the community colleges trying to do everything. Legislators don't really want mass education. And then comes the comment, "Granted that the state legislatures do not understand the community college well, the problem may be even more acute with the federal government."

Obviously there is need to improve communication between community college representatives and state legislators. An awareness of that was registered in a recent survey to determine priorities as perceived by college and university presidents.[1] Ranked first by the community college respondents was, "communicating our strengths to the legislature."

S. I. Hayakawa, who achieved a good deal of recognition for his work in the field of semantics before becoming a U.S. senator, has written about problems in communication. His comments can be helpful. The symbol is not the thing symbolized; the word is not the thing; the map is not the territory it stands for. Hayakawa probably would not say that a top need is to find better ways of *communicating our strengths* to state legislatures or finance officers. He would say what we need to do is to bring into closer relationship the verbal world, the map, and the world that people know through their own experience, the territory. The word "college" is a map, it may bear little resemblance to the territory.

> Similarly, by means of imaginary or false reports, or by false references from good reports, or by mere rhetorical exercises, we can manufacture at will, with language, "maps" which have no reference to the extensional world. Here again no harm will be done unless someone makes the mistake of regarding such "maps" as representing real territories.[2]

Experience in the "territory" of community colleges gives one the impression of significant individual and social benefits. The map, the word, needs somehow to represent that reality. Strategies can be developed to bring that about. They must be developed *if* the map is to be used by the traveler, in this case by legislators enacting policy and taxpayers providing support and learners deciding whether to use the institution.

A president followed that line of reason when he said that the legislature doesn't really have an awareness of community colleges—so we need to do more than lobby. We need to find ways to relate to these people so that the community college is intellectually more interesting to them. We need to help them understand that this institution is different.

The Political Arena

There are other people in the state who are committed to the same cause—to help the legislature understand that their institution is different. Community college representatives are not naive about politics. In the local setting the realities of the political process are omnipresent; "local knowledge" is one of the administrator's most useful tools. Without separating from the local scene, however, presidents and boards find that a good part of the action is now in the state capital and the stage and players are different. There is a new reality that requires new roles. That fact became very clear to me one afternoon in Springfield, Illinois. I wanted to talk to a person who was serving her eighth term in the House of Representatives. She had been one of the co-sponsors of the Community College Act in 1965. To contact the legislator, it was necessary for me to hand my card to one of the ushers at the door to the chamber. The card was then delivered to her and she eventually came to the corridor to talk with me. We talked about adult education and community colleges. Her parting words were—"Sometimes I am amazed at the dream world in which higher education people are living. They just don't seem to know the real world out there."

I thought of those words as I pressed through the crowd of people, lobbyists, standing at the door of the chamber and sending their cards in. The corridor was filled with hundreds of coal miners. In fact, in front of the capitol there were some 2,000 miners, described by the press as being angry miners. They were holding up placards, one of them saying, "EPA is O.K. but it don't pay" (Environmental Protection Act). Another, "Save Our Jobs." These were members of the United Mineworkers. Another little placard down in the main corridor of the State Capitol called for support for ERA (Equal Rights Amendment). Like it or not, circumstances have led community colleges to the state capitols. Legislative perceptions cannot be ignored.

How Do Perceptions Differ from Proposals?

Perception: Education is for the young.

Response: Education needs to be lifelong. Already a large part of the adult population is participating in educational activities. Policies need to acknowledge that.

Perception: The numbers of education will be declining.

Response: The numbers of people in the age cohort 18-24 will decline. Educational interests and needs of citizens of all ages will continue to grow.

Perception: Education is for occupation, college degree, and "remediation."

Response: Education needs to be related to all of life's "stages," and to those elements of life that go beyond work— literature, arts, music, crafts, those learning experiences that keep meaning in life.

Perception: Competition is increasing among educational providers.

Response: The community college will be part of an integrated system of community services.

---

[1] National Center for Higher Education Management Systems. ''Management Needs Assessment Survey.'' Boulder: the Center, 1979.

[2] S. I. Hayakawa. *Language in Thought and Action*. New York: Harcourt, Brace, and Company, 1949, p. 33.

Chapter VI

WHO PAYS? FOR WHAT?

Anew reality demands redesign of America's automobiles. Gone are the days when a dollar bought five gallons of gasoline or a 10 dollar purchase would fill the tank. The morning news had its usual affront to the digestive system with the prophecy that, before the eighties become history, gasoline might be selling for 10 dollars a gallon. So the big, fast, over-stuffed denizen of the interstates and freeways is fast yielding to a vehicle appropriate to the changed circumstances. Change, perhaps as radical, is required in education. We need both a more efficient "vehicle" and different bases upon which "fuel" is made available. Community college education suffers from "cultural lag" in methods of financial support. Money is distributed to institutions largely in terms suitable to another era when education was to prepare for life and to equip the young to "move out into the world."

A Cost-Sensitive Environment

To discuss financing without demonstrating awareness of significant changes in the economic environment is to be as foolhardy as a mariner who fails to take cloud formations into account. First, inflation is a fact. Its force is altering our society and is bound to have continuing affect upon community colleges. Further, we have already acknowledged the problem of other mounting special costs. "What will it cost?" has become a pervading question in the shaping of educational policy at the state level. Many legislators see little prospect for substantial increase in financial resources. Indeed, the major question is likely to be one of reallocation of existing resources in terms of new orders of priority.

So important has become the financial element that there may be developing, by default of those who carry responsibilities to determine ends, a new order of "fiscal-philosophers." "How does one construct aid formulas until one answers that question of mission?", said one budget official. "Obviously, it has changed since the 1960's. One of the biggest frustrations I have is tying budgets into missions." And from another:

> The budget office has a role to play, but there has been a tendency, because we review budgets, to assume that we have programmatic responsibilities. There is a tendency to attribute more authority to us than we have or should have. It's not our role, really, to deal with mission. We are not initiators. We go down a different track. But we sure as hell will have to have some answers to this matter of mission.

Previously we have described how community colleges have changed over the last 10 years and have suggested that changes of similar importance have taken place in the organization and functions of state legislatures. Now another related factor should be noted; shifts in taxing methods that have the effect of increasing the proportion of income and disbursals at the state level. Proposition 13 in California is the best known example of transferring obligations to the state level that were formerly borne by local jurisdictions. In other states, less dramatic moves have taken place with somewhat similar effects. An industrialist heading up a committee to study community college finance described the process in his state:

> . . . it turned out that the local districts were putting in perhaps 60 percent or more. Then the income tax was adopted in 1969 in order to try to provide more revenue for the state and following that they took personal property tax off the individual—this was in 1973 and this was never replaced. Now there is this corporate personal property tax which is being discontinued. It will have to be replaced but this means that funds rather than being available locally on the direct

117

basis will now go the state treasury and be distributed from the state treasury. So now we (local areas) lose control of that kind of money.

In canvassing elements that could influence the shaping of state policy for financing community colleges, another factor should be noted—the problem of "open-endedness." Legislators have demonstrated concern about fiscal measures that leave open the possible level of state obligation. Thus, a "cap" was placed on community college enrollments in California in 1973 after state officials observed a substantial growth in enrollments as the result of what they perceived to be expansion of community colleges into adult education. A fiscal analyst in Michigan reported similar developments in 1976 which led to changes in community college funding. Michigan had been in its worst recession since depression days. In 1975 and 1976 there was a 20 percent compounded increase in enrollments in community colleges. Until then, financing had been somewhat open-ended. As enrollments went up, appropriations rose. In that period there were two $5 million supplemental appropriations required. The community colleges were no longer small potatoes. They had grown in just a short time from using about $50 million to $100 million of state money. In 1976-77, the legislature took away 50 percent of the appropriations for leisure courses and totally eliminated that support the following year.

State officials are rightly concerned about developments in the colleges which, in effect, commit the state to sign a blank check. Community college officials express similar concern about actions at the state level which place mounting obligations upon the colleges. Funding provisions may be categorical but turn out to be less than full cost. A group of presidents described tasks taken on over the last 15 years:

> Remediation, child care, career centers, financial aid, veterans, EOPs (Educational Opportunity Programs), handicapped services— for example, vans, wheelchairs, affirmative action for students. At the time this was all right because assessed valuations were increasing, but all the time we were adding on tasks rather than prioritizing. Now we must drop some things. It's suicide to drop services to these groups. They are well-organized. The blacks, the veterans, the people in child care know how to get to the state capitol.

Sensitivity to cost factors is a phenomenon not limited to state legislators and budget officials. Administrators and local trustees share in the dilemmas.

Against this background of such factors as inflation, cost concerns, mission ambiguities, and change in tax sources, what are the problems and issues that are illustrative in financing community colleges' services within a policy for lifelong education?

It is not my intention, incidentally, to propose new financing formulas in detail nor to deal with a comprehensive list of money issues. Frankly, I do not know what the best methods would be in the various states. That is one reason I have helped to encourage the attention of economists and foundations to the complex questions inherent in devising financial policies that facilitate rather than impede the distinctive functions of community colleges. Along with many others, I will be looking forward in 1980 to the results of an intensive study of these matters by the Brookings Institution, directed by economists David Breneman and Susan Nelson. My efforts here are to highlight problem areas and to identify some factors that require attention in any such studies.

Credit Hour Deficient

The limitations of credit hour production as the key element in funding formulas have been stated in a report published by the Illinois Board of Higher Education:

> The credit hour, the most commonly used unit in funding formulas, provides a reasonably standard measure of educational effort among traditional programs, but its use creates problems for many non-traditional programs. Programs such as non-credit competency-based programs, individualized modules, learning contract arrangements and off-campus learning may be under-funded because they have difficulty in competing when funding is based upon a formula that does not fit their offerings . . .

If such programs are held to be non-traditional, then a good deal of community college work is non-traditional and what is said about the deficiencies of the credit-hour measure applies. Similar statements come out of California and are even more critical of current financial patterns:

> The existing fiscal structure for community colleges is designed for a system analogous to the 6th grade education of an 11-year old. In California, this student attends school 175 days per year and is expected to spend all of his or her time, each day, in the immediate presence of an instructor.

In California the unit of measurement for state level reimbursement is average daily attendance, with the requirement that it be under the supervision of an instructor. As was pointed out to me—institutions are supported on the basis of the utilization of seat time. For funding purposes, what matters is how long the student occupies the chair, not what the student does in that time. Nor does the existing system encourage adaptation to changing circumstances.

> Statutory restrictions on the community colleges' academic calendar, course scheduling, and the way student activity is measured for funding purposes (the classroom contact hour) hinder the ability of colleges to experiment with instruction that can serve their clientele more effectively. These statutes discourage and, in some cases, literally prevent efforts to utilize (a) modular rather than traditional-length terms and (b) variable length or open entry-open exit classes based upon mastery of specific course components. Likewise, programmed learning, independent study, ITV and other techniques (such as credit for prior and/or extra-college experience) which do not require the typical amount of direct contact between students and faculty are discouraged. This occurs in spite of the fact that such techniques may enable faculty to educate students at less cost than the traditional lecture or lab. Solutions to these and other problems require remedial legislation.

Without question, there are marked differences between the kinds of learners envisioned under the existing fiscal arrangements and those described in a report cited earlier—"continuing education for part-time, adult students has become the dominant function of the community colleges."

A legislative study criticized the existing funding formula in Michigan because of its rigidity in basing state appropriations only upon credit hour production. The study noted:

> The cost factors used in the formula appeared to bear little resemblance to the actual costs reported by the colleges to the state, and the actual cost data was subject to so much institutional interpretation in its generation that comparisons were regarded as less than meaningful.

The need for a reporting structure which addressed the unique features of community colleges was first expressed as a goal by the legislature in Enrolled Senate Bill 1346, which established a task force to develop alternatives for funding community college education. In working toward a new funding formula, the following legislative objectives were set forth:

1. To establish a funding formula which is need based, building upon criteria acceptable to the colleges and the state.
2. To recognize institutional uniqueness without creating a formula which encourages political manipulation.
3. To separately identify and fund fixed and variable costs to minimize the hazardous impact of rapid enrollment fluctuations.
4. To recognize output variables other than credit hours which influence institutional costs (such as head count, use of learning labs, etc.)
5. To minimize the educational disparities caused by large variations in the property tax base of the college districts.
6. To provide state decision makers with a sound framework for prioritizing the funding of educational roles.
7. To take into consideration the costs associated with meeting the various objectives of an educational institution.
8. To provide a better long-range budgeting framework.
9. To permit the continuation of local board autonomy in educational decisions.

Reference is made above to "head count" as a variable which can influence institutional costs. Head count in community colleges is increasing at a faster rate than the number of full-time equivalent students. Funding formulas may not take this into account. Administrative costs rise with the number of learners as do the expenses of operating and maintaining facilities and of providing student services such as counseling. Often, however, financial support is tied to FTE's. In one state, the ratio of fiscal year equated students to head count in the community colleges rose from 1.51 to 1.73 in a 10-year period. In other words, it now takes 17.3 head count students to generate 100 FYES, the basis of support. During that same period the ratio changed from 1.0 to 1.1 in the baccalaureate and private institutions of that state. Until 1979, the formula dealt only with credit hours and was related to FYES, not the actual number of students. Clearly, community colleges were disadvantaged under that system because of the high proportion of part-time students enrolled.

Another serious deficiency in funding, based only on production of credits or on enrollments, is the absence of incentives and resources to develop liaison with other community organizations in the provision of educational services. Nor is there recognition of the necessity for continuing assessments of educational needs and interests in the college district. Both functions, we have said, are essential elements to the community college mission.

Can Local Flexibility Be Maintained?

It is highly desirable for community colleges to have local funds available as well as financial support from the state. Flexibility and quick responsiveness are facilitated by local determinations. Legislators have indicated repeatedly that the college could do whatever it wished with local resources. The state's concern appears to be with those programs for which state funds are utilized. Since there is an evident trend toward receipt of a greater proportion of support from the state level, one could infer that the element of local determination is becoming less significant. Fiscal experts in some states, aware of that prospect, warn community college leadership of the probable consequences. Was a state-level financial officer exaggerating when he said that the community colleges in his state were at a critical threshold? He maintained that if the state puts in the majority of the dollars, the institutions will likely lose their flexibility, as well as local control, and their freedom to explore. He would urge the institutions to avoid sacrificing flexibility and control for a broad, state-assured financial base. He suggested economies in operation as well as seeking other recourses as alternatives to becoming part of a state-wide system.

In another state, budget people noted that questions are being raised locally about the fiscal burden. There may be a push for the state to take over and become the primary sponsor. We are accustomed, they said, to engaging in detailed budgeting and budget analysis. There would seem to be some natural accretion of power at the state levels which might be seen as a willing trade-off of flexibility for sustained support.

An authority in yet another state favored a lump sum appropriation which would cover costs of transfer, technical, and remediation programs. The remaining services would be determined locally and financed through a local tax. He pointed out how communities differ, and, consequently, how the benefits of discretionary funds are important.

Most community college people would agree that local tax resources are desirable, but, realistically, what are the options? Property tax, the long-time source of revenues for education, has been under attack throughout the nation. It is possible that the pendulum could swing back at least partially if people recognize that there is a high price to pay for state funding in terms of diminishing local autonomy.

A sales tax has an interesting limitation as it relates to community college support. Community colleges could be described as counter-cyclical. As the economy declines, the enrollments go up. As the economy improves, enrollment may decline. The surge in enrollment in Michigan in 1975-76, when the state was experiencing a financial depression, should not have come as a surprise to the legislators. One college reports in its analysis of the period from 1970 to 1978 that the most direct cause-effect impactor on enrollment was the employment rate in its district. Numerous community college leaders concur that the greatest single predictor of credit hour enrollments is the community employment rate. Where more people are working full-time and overtime the less time thay have to commit to college studies. What is the problem, then, with sales tax revenues? Obviously, when unemployment is high, sales will lag along with tax revenues. Yet, needs of the college increase as enrollments rise.

Regardless of what the sources of revenue will be, there is a good deal of impressive opinion to the effect that institutional flexibility and control are furthered by the injection of local dollars.

What About the "Soft" Areas?

Major debates about community college funding, as has been noted, tend to revolve around the "soft" areas which often are part of community or public service offerings. In fact, discussions about macrame or fly-tying and belly dancing sometimes have reached such a feverish pitch as to cause "legislation by anecdote." The phenomenon is a familiar one. A legislator may hear from some constituent that the local college is offering a course in "Beach Combing for Senior Citizens." Without further ado, the legislative machine is cranked up, and a bill is introduced which may have the effect of sharply reducing the number of "taxpayer-supported" college programs for senior citizens. Unfortunately, the intensity of debate over avocational learning pursuits, hobbies, and leisure programs frequently has obscured a basic issue: Is it good public policy to encourage and facilitate learning throughout life? Having determined the answer to that question, then the appropriate and derivative question follows: Who should pay for what kinds of services?

A further negative effect of these arguments has been that they have conditioned perceptions of many community services as whimsical and limited to satisfying personal interests. Consequently, financial support has been adversely affected for services often vital to community life. An example of this is found in the earlier description of the key role played by Waubonsee Community College in development of housing rehabilitation programs. For more than four years, the college has been involved in addressing the educational component of housing problems in its service area. The results are impressive: the number of low interest rehabilitation loans were increased, conventional mortgage loans were made in areas where formerly they were not available, and local government has invested large sums in community development block grant capital improvements. Recorded property purchases rose substantially, which would indicate there has been much reinvestment in the neighborhood.

Subsequently, the need for rehabilitation of older housing in the cities and the close-in suburbs throughout the state has been emphasized by the "Task Force on the Future of Illinois." Efforts of Waubonsee apparently have been effective in responding to a need stipulated to be of high priority statewide. The manner in which higher education funds are distributed in the state, however, limits the degree to which Waubonsee and other community colleges can attack such problems. No higher education funds were available to underwrite college costs in the work which led to the formation of Neighborhood Housing Services of Aurora, the Waubonsee district, because the educational services could not be measured in terms of traditional credit hours. Now, when the college is offering credit courses in housing rehabilitation, reimbursement for those credit hours is less than 50 percent of the rate at which funding is provided for training, for example, of prospective elementary school teachers.

Community colleges in Illinois are financed much like those in many other states. There are three major sources of support:

1. Tuition.
2. Local real estate taxes.
3. Reimbursement from the state of Illinois in proportion to the *number of credit hours generated*.

Courses and programs are divided into six categories:

1. Baccalaureate programs.
2. Health occupational programs.
3. Technical occupational programs.
4. Business occupational programs.
5. General studies (includes developmental and remedial).
6. Public services (community education and community service).

The first four categories are fully funded at the rate of reimbursement determined by the state formula. General studies are funded at 50 percent. Public service activities are not funded at all by the state, although there is a factor which theoretically "frees up" local tax money to be used to "meet unique local needs."

Policy issues similar to those in Illinois exist in other states as well. What are the assumptions upon which the present funding arrangements are based? Do the assumptions imply that continuing education and community services are locally oriented and therefore ought to be funded by local resources? Is the state interest properly centered on the occupational and transfer programs? A state-wide task force has identified urgent issues to be dealt with by the state's citizenry during the next decade in such fields as agriculture, jobs/growth, energy, health/human resources, work force, and environment. These are state-wide concerns. Under existing fiscal policies, community colleges are limited in their response through "non-traditional" educational programs. Should such programs have a lesser priority for state dollars than the baccalaureate and occupational offerings? The details of any funding formulas are not as important as the policy position taken. The purposes for which money is provided tend to determine the direction of institutions to a greater degree than do assessments of educational needs and interests in the community. Fiscal policies have the power to shape the institutions and to determine their missions.

It was recognition of the influence of fiscal policies that led a college dean to write to a state senator about the possible effects of existing policies:

> Stating this point in another way, in times of limited resources and tight budgets, local Boards of Trustees and administrations realize that they can generate more income from state reimbursement by investing local revenue in baccalaureate and occupational programs for which the state will reimburse 100% of differential cost. Therefore we train more teachers and liberal arts majors, who may not obtain unsubsidized employment for which they were trained, and we do not train moderate and low income people to rehabilitate housing.

Earlier it was said that a primary function of community colleges is to aid those who want to learn how to secure basic necessities such as housing, health, employment, food, and citizenship rights and responsibilities. Such learning, to be effective, may take place in forms and places quite different from those for traditional education. Semesters, credits, campuses, and other academic gear, along with determinants of financial support based upon this nomenclature, will need to give way to approaches more appropriate to the needs and styles of new learners.

Need for Description and Data

From the clouds of confusion and mixed perceptions over the "soft" areas a number of lessons emerge. For example, it has been found useful to define the terms. It helps to describe the programs. And good data may shorten the time required for discussion.

In March of 1979, the Michigan Senate acknowledged the importance of obtaining better information to accurately assess the financial needs of community colleges. The community college appropriations act for FY79 included the following section:

> The Department of Management and Budget, in cooperation with the Senate fiscal agency, the House fiscal agency, the Department of Education, and the community colleges shall begin development of a community college program classification structure for use in documenting financial needs of community colleges. Uniform application of accounting principles shall be employed in the collection of cost data.

The former six categories of programs for funding purposes have now been replaced by 15. Community education instruction includes home and family life/human development, and personal interest. Distinctions have been made between activities that equip the learner to function more effectively in society and those that are for personal "consumption." Inasmuch as a good deal of heat is generated over the question of what should be considered an appropriate use of tax funds, it is interesting to examine the area of home and family life/human development as compared with the category of "personal interest":

> Home and family life instruction is defined as learning strategies designed to provide the learner with knowledge, skills and capabilities related to the establishment, maintenance, and improvement of a home; to the carrying out of those functions typically associated with the conduct of a household; or to the person's responsibilities as a member of the family unit. This category includes those offerings that focus on the person's role as a worker, member of a social organization. In addition, those instructional offerings that provide the learner with knowledge, skills, and background needed to function more effectively as an individual or to interact with the variety of social institutions.

Personal interest instruction is defined as:

. . . learning strategies designed to support an individual's recreational or avocational pursuits or to improve his or her day-to-day living skills. The activities included in this category focus on the individual as user of leisure time rather than upon the individual as a member of a social institution or upon occupational and career-related needs. Personal interest instruction is defined as learning strategies designed to provide opportunities for persons seeking immediate pleasure, satisfaction or relaxation during their leisure time. Students who enroll do so for the purpose of exploring, developing, or refining hobby or handicraft skills or participating in organized forms of play.

In addition to fields of instruction, including those described above, there is provision for public service as well as other categories of operations. The public service program includes those "program elements established to make available to the public the various unique resources and capabilities of the institutions with the specific purpose of responding to a community need or solving a community problem."

There will continue to be differences of opinion with regard to the kinds of educational services appropriate to state funding and, indeed, the determination of appropriateness may vary over time with state priorities. Basic to any determination of policy, however, is the need for a clear description of the learning activities to be conducted as well as accurate and uniform data reports.

The Problem of Cost-Effectiveness

How do you make a case for the value to the state of educational services that help people to rehabilitate their houses, become better parents, participate proficiently in government, improve their health, and continue to maintain themselves in society as they grow older? Can it be demonstrated that such education is cost effective? As one listens to many people discuss the future of the community college, there is a note that is sounded repeatedly. How do we prove the worth of programs to which we are committed—non-credit parent education, for example, or educational services in nursing homes? After all these are decisions on values so what kind of foundation can be established for policy determination? On what grounds do we persuade policy makers that a good part of what they may see as "soft" areas are relevant and growth-stimulating? These worries and occasional doubts of community college people must be answered if a sense of community college mission is to emerge and gain acceptance. Measuring "cost-effectiveness" is a difficult task. In non-traditional areas it is especially troublesome because, eventually, it becomes a matter of social judgment. Some persons would justify almost any course, no matter how trivial it would appear to be. Others would be extremely critical of the same offering. There is little consensus on values as one moves out to the uncharted areas of community learning. Until an instrument can be designed and applied to ascertain the effects of various kinds of services in the community, final answers will not be reached on the proper amalgam of the community college as college, learning center, and activities center. Impact studies are needed to provide a better basis for determinations of worth and, hence, suitable public investment.

Intentions and interest need to be translated into fact-finding. For example, the vice-chairman of a community college board told me that it would be interesting to look into the employment problems of black youth and then look at the employment record of the black graduates of that college. It was his impression that most of the latter had jobs. He said it would be interesting to get the figures on these. But why doesn't he have the figures? He who lacks good information in these data-oriented times is seriously handicapped. Said the chairman of a state board, "A case needs to be made for those we serve. The needs require documentation." And he added, "They certainly must not be outlandish in cost."

And, declared a president, a systematic program evaluation is required at his institution, especially to deal with long-range considerations. He said that college officials did not really know whether their programs were meeting objectives. One-third of the students are in the vocational field. Forty-five percent of the programs are vocational. What is happening, he wanted to know. How do we get better information for decision making and how do we make this information available to policy makers?

In the vocational field is this such a difficult task?

Another institution had data. They told me, "More than half of our students are on welfare. Fifty-five percent of the students are from families who have an income of $5,000 or less per year. After students leave us, 55 percent make over $10,000 per year. Over 20 percent make between $15,000 and $20,000. In other words, many of them have tripled their income and 97 percent continue to live in the city after their training." That statement gets close to making a case for cost-effectiveness when the public investment is factored in.

Another way to approach the cost-effect question is in terms of preventative fiscal costs to the community. After reporting on the total cost of the Parent Education Programs in San Francisco, the college cited costs of remedial measures which the community was saved through preventative programs:

1. Juvenile residential care cost a minimum of $650/month to maintain one person.
2. Institutional care was a minimum of $1000-$1200/month to maintain one person.
3. If there is psychiatric care involved, the cost for one person is a minimum of $1500/month.
4. Additionally, counseling for one person costs city agencies $1200/year for three contact hours per week. This includes counseling for delinquency, drug abuse, alcoholism, and others.

The difficulties in establishing a direct line between public investment and cost effectiveness or benefits is illustrated in the experience of a student in a California community college. He was the student member of the board of trustees. I had interviewed the board about their views on the essential elements in community college mission. The student said that his own experiences would illustrate what he hoped the community college would continue to do for people.

He first started to work toward a doctorate through a premedical course at the University of California at Irvine. He left after three years, deciding it wasn't for him. He then went to the community college with the intent of getting a bachelor's degree. He planned to take the lower division business course and then transfer to a four-year college. But he found he was not particularly interested in the degree. His father-in-law was in the construction business so he decided that he would prepare for that field. Not particularly degree-oriented, he wanted to take the courses that would be useful to him in the construction business. As far as he was concerned, he commented, he'll probably use the college as long as he lives. It was his view that college work becomes "addictive."

How do we determine the student's objective and whether it has been met? How do we calculate the costs and the effects and benefits? Clearly, he isn't through with the college. It may not be construction, but possibly some other interest that will bring him back again. Are those interests legitimate? How do we determine that? Should the state pay? What frame of reference do we use? Note that he had taken three years of college work before he came to the community college. The state already had made an investment in him. An additional factor may be overlooked. Both he and his business are contributors to tax revenues.

Obviously, calculating cost-effectiveness upon the basis of a two-year program that culminates in an associate degree will be an inadequate measure. Then do we try to make judgments of results based upon student intention? That may be difficult to identify. Commented a president:

> We define our mission. We define our objectives. Then we go ahead and try to define student goals. For example, a student wants typing and we say, therefore, that her goal is the secretarial field. But we didn't ask her. She may only want a couple of courses and then wants to go to work but now we define her as a dropout and she becomes a part of the statistic that says, you don't have many completers. We seem obliged to keep the score in some simple-minded units. We are forced to be bean counters.

Other budget people say you cannot focus on student intent because you cannot really find out what it is. In one state, funding now is based upon the purpose for which the course is offered as that described in a brochure or the catalogue. For example, Spanish for people who are going to merely travel in Spain is probably not structured and requires no syllabus. It would be different from Spanish for those who are going to learn it more in depth. However, it is not considered advisable to differentiate on the basis of credit or non-credit. If you do that, a budget officer observed, there is a tendency for all courses to become credit and we find some institutions with no non-credit courses. And non-credit courses may be of equal value to credit in terms of the objectives of many learners.

Fiscal officers acknowledge a tension between student objectives and their areas of financial responsibility:

> Actually, the average student in community colleges does not complete his program in two years. He or she may stay a longer time in order to accomplish personal objectives. This drives up the cost and it really drives up average expenditures.

As we observe participants in community college programs, these are among the educational characteristics which have implications for methods of financial support: Learners have a broad spectrum of objectives that range from personal interests to occupational goals. Objectives change over the course of time. Learners tend to maintain relationships with the college that extend well beyond a two-year period although the contacts may be sporadic. Learners are inclined to take parts or pieces of programs. Proportionately few of them are recipients of the associate degree. On the other hand, a growing number have the equivalent of more than two years of college experience.

These are among the factors which must be taken into account as grounds are established for the funding and the evaluating of these institutions.

One possible approach to resolving problems and issues of finance and mission is to consider where the *major* foci of responsibility lie for meeting community learning needs. If functional literacy, general education, and basic skills are primarily federal and state responsibilities, for example, then the mechanisms for finance and evaluation in this area must operate at central state levels. But if occupational, vocational, technical, professional, manpower, and other employment-based learning needs are responsibilities of both local and state groups, then finance and evaluation mechanisms must be shared on a cooperative basis. On the other hand, community learning needs that might be described as personal and leisure can be financed and evaluated locally, perhaps by individual boards, not by the state. These considerations are essential in developing a finance policy for lifelong education.

But fiscal support for learning is scarce. Appropriations are not to be (and cannot be) viewed as available in "blank check" form to cover all learning needs. One of the most critical implications for the finance policy framework is that, in a system of scarce resources, allocation decisions become increasingly political. Questions of whose learning has priority, and where dollar support subsequently flows, become social issues in the political arena as much as in the educational arena. Scarce money forces both politicians and educators to make new choices.

Community colleges thus have a new opportunity in the 1980's to participate in the political process of setting local, state, and federal priorities for learning. Careful and thoughtful consideration of its mission—by each college—can enrich this process and result in more responsible finance policy. If the priorities were to develop further toward federal and state support for "remedial" education, and if fiscal support were to follow, for example, then the college must consider two implications. First would be the possibility of an increased federal and state role in regulation and evaluation of remedial learning, and the governance and accountability changes which would be necessary. The second implication would be that of a probable shift to the local level of other priorities, such as local economic development or personal learning. The implications of these priorities for the local level can also be considered in advance. Colleges could retain their valuable flexibility and rapid responses to new needs emerging in their communities. And fiscal support, governance issues, and evaluation of local priorities could be retained locally. Furthermore, local groups could invest in their *own* priorities, while at the same time providing additional remedial learning opportunity consistent with state and federal priorities. The finance policy implications suggest a framework where each priority is supported, with dollars, by its source. For the community college, the strength of a policy structure which segregates fiscal responsibility among various sectors, and follows their priorities, is that it also helps segregate important new political questions into appropriate arenas for discussion and decision.

A More Efficient "Vehicle"

In the introduction to this chapter it was asserted that there was need for different bases upon which funds are made available to community colleges. Also specified as a need was a more efficient "vehicle." Along with greater proportions of financial support from the state level has come increased interest of state bodies in the management capabilities and the accountability efforts of the local institutions. Without question, board members will be required to demonstrate their capacity to be accountable for both their fiscal and educational stewardship. To assure that, superior management must be required by the board. A great deal more hangs on this matter than solvency or satisfactory audits. Involved is a basic element in community college philosophy—the assumption that people at the local level can become proficient in dealing with problems that affect their lives. As we shall see in the next chapter, that tenet is under serious question.

And more will be said about management in the chapter on "leadership." It is enough now to review briefly previous references to ways in which colleges that encourage and facilitate learning in their communities can extend their means. For example, coordination with the efforts of other institutions to consolidate resources and possibly trim costs is one important means. Community colleges through a cooperative stance have frequently broadened their resource base. Further, many colleges have expanded their capital significantly by utilization of "clinical settings." And it should not be overlooked that community agencies, business, industry, and the labor unions all have budgets, staff, facilities, boards and advisory groups, as well as funds designated for education and training. Granted that demands are many, all of these represent possible resources that can supplement state appropriations for educational programs.

What Happens When Charges Rise?

During the 1960's and early '70's, "low cost" and "close-to-home" were commonly identified as the two most influential factors in motivating learners to choose the community college. In a number of states and metropolitan areas, no tuition was charged. And in others, student charges were minimal. Now that picture is changing rapidly. Presently only in California is enrollment tuition-free. In New York State during the year 1979, provisions were under consideration which would permit a maximum tuition of $900 in the 30 community colleges under the State University of New York and would match the freshman-sophomore cost at the state-operated four-year campuses. Further, funds are provided in New York and other states for students to go to private institutions. So the question arises as to whether cost to the student will be of less importance in attracting students to community colleges in the future. Another related development during the past several years, of course, has been that of the massive increase in financial assistance from federal programs. At one institution visited, 91 percent of the students were getting financial aid, including state and local scholarship funds. There does appear to be a continuing belief that it is cheaper to go to a community college. This could be called a psychological differentiating factor. Many students say there is a lot of hassle involved in getting financial aid. They don't like to fill out the forms. Not all people are motivated sufficiently or have the expertise to explore all the means that might be available. So, they say, it is much better just to come to the community college.

At the federal level, as well as in the states, efforts are continuing to open up eligibility for financial aid to persons taking less than half-time courses for independent students—those who are no longer living with their parents.

What happens when charges to the students increase? Nobody seems to be sure. Studies of possible effects have been made in four-year colleges but the population of community colleges is different and may be much more sensitive to cost factors. There is considerable supposition, particularly with regard to non-credit programs, such as parent education, labor studies, and arts programs, about the effects of increasing the price. A common view is that the people who can afford it will be there. And the gap will widen between the "haves" and the "have-nots." In her review of significant major studies of adult learners, Patricia Cross hypothesizes that finances are not the key to the access question. She suggests that the real problems relate to motivation, previous educational experience, and other factors. If you really want to get at the problem, according to Dr. Cross, you ought to put a lot of money into information services. There is enough money available if counseling and information services are comprehensive. People need to know what the price is for certain kinds of programs, whether they are for credit or not, and what the alternatives might be.[1]

Clearly, this problem of costs requires careful and sustained attention. Is it true, as some suspect, that financial constraints drive institutions back to more traditional behavior? If the cost to the learner must rise substantially to offset declining tax funds for community services and continuing education, will certain programs lose their clientele? Although the results may have been more short-term than long, an impact study on the effects of Proposition 13 on community services was summarized as "Last in, first out." "Programs of community services and those designed to serve new clienteles seem to be the ones that are cut back when the financial chips are down."

We cannot afford to base planning and policy development on conjecture and supposition. We need to know much more about relationships between educational prices and participation rates. Why? Because our thesis is that there are educational services which are among life's necessities, not its luxuries. Such services need to be available throughout life in much the same way as those in the field of health. Society is giving a great deal of attention to creating equitable and effective lifelong programs for medical care—and how to pay for them. A similar acknowledgement is required of the essential nature of educational services throughout a lifetime.

Will the Means Be Supplied?

How realistic is it to talk about adapting financial policies to a concept of lifelong education? Some would think this is not a good time to be raising such questions. We might be better off to settle for the way things are and hope we can hold on. One thing is sure, those who are interested in change cannot afford to be naive or to behave like Pollyannas. "What will it cost" tends to be a question that almost immediately surfaces in any discussion of proposed action. It pops up like a cork to quickly block out such reasonable questions as "What is desirable" and "What is feasible?" The chairman of the senate finance committee in a state legislature expressed concerns about that:

> We are dealing with the problem of how to live in an age of austerity for the public sector. It's not so much a matter of what our educational needs are but what can we spend, and we need to evaluate community colleges in the context of a nation that is developing a new value system which is hedonistic and materialistic.

Some observers wonder whether perhaps that value system may not be changing to one somewhat less materialistic. An international authority on adult education, who had recently conducted studies in the United States, expressed his sobering assessment to me:

> There was a powerful liberal wind blowing in the United States in the 1960's and now there are countervailing forces and people talk angrily about the failure of poverty programs and now they tend to blame the poor. There is a good deal of backlash thinking.

Interestingly, in almost the same breath he reported the tendency for the analogue of the U.S. community college to be appearing elsewhere in the world. Developing countries, he said, are establishing institutions of a similar nature, locally-based and relating to local needs.

A *New York Times* survey in mid-1979 reported that the trend toward reducing or repealing taxes and imposing spending limits on state and local governments has been a strong and pervasive one, with virtually all of the states curtailing revenues or spending or both in some fashion. And the report indicated that the tax revolt shows no sign of abating. Moreover, it is stated:

> Overall, the state actions were primarily intended to benefit the broad sector of middle-class citizens who have been protesting in recent years about the tax burden, and commercial interests that have long maintained powerful lobbies in state capitols and have capitalized on the middle-class protest.[2]

One more dose of pessimism comes from across the seas. I asked an adult educational leader in London why education was not perceived as a resource to be used by the United Kingdom in dealing with numerous social and economic problems which we had discussed. She speculated that education had promised too much in recent years, that it was not able to deliver. The consequence was that people were first disappointed and then disillusioned. Unemployment, inflation, crime, and family disorganization continued to prevail. She felt that the prospects for supporting adult education were not bright. And she added another comment which may be of extraordinary significance: how difficult and sometimes unsuccessful was the process through which institutions change to match societal requirements.

Granted that there are social facts with which we must deal. What does analysis of our experience reveal to us? What have we learned? It may appear simplistic but there is evidence that very often the approach of educational institutions has been to do things *for* people rather than *with* them. On the contrary, we have sought to describe in these pages a stance of "symbiosis"—"the living together of two dissimilar organisms in close association or union, especially where this is advantageous to both, as distinguished from parasitism." These are the kinds of considerations that illustrate such a relationship:

- If we are concerned about the rising costs to support large numbers of dependent people, does it not make sense to consider what can be done to help them become productive, contributing citizens?
- Would it not be in the self-interest of the nation and our communities for its citizens to be self-sufficient, self-supporting, and able to contribute for as long as possible?
- An argument for suitable education and training for employment, disease prevention, and "positive aging" is to ease the load of the taxpayer by proportionately reducing the numbers who are limited in paying their own way.
- It is a primary function of community colleges to aid those in the community who want to learn how to secure basic necessities. Among these are: housing, health, employment, food, and citizenship rights and responsibilities.

These postulates speak of "association which is advantageous to both." They deal with the "basics." Obviously education is not limited to these pragmatic matters. It can send people soaring far above the bread and butter issues—and it should. But its flight will be short and labored unless it touches these areas of basic and primary concern. That is where keys can be found for the resources we need.

---

[1] K. Patricia Cross. *Beyond the Open Door*. San Francisco: Jossey-Bass, 1974

[2] John Herbers. *The New York Times*, August 5, 1979, p. 38.

Chapter VII

QUESTIONS AND ISSUES OF CONTROL

If we were to telephone 50 community college presidents today and ask, "What do you consider the most troublesome issue in your work at this time?", the answer might be "money," or even "energy," but the odds are strongly in favor of its being "loss of institutional control." Presidents and local trustees perceive power is flowing from local jurisdictions to the state level. And they reveal frustration at carrying the burdens of accountability even as more decisions affecting local operations appear to be made in the state capitals. "But the state has to have more say," declare members of the legislature, "the state has to draw some lines. We have to ask what are the state priorities in funding community colleges. When the state provides a billion dollars for postsecondary education, there must be some accountability. At least, the necessity is not going to go away."

No issue generates more heat in discussion at this time than that of the control of community colleges and questions of who makes decisions. Who has authority? An institution which in its developmental years was largely governed in the local setting, and which traditionally assigned a strong administrative role to the president or superintendent, finds that authority for decision making has shown some tendencies to accompany the dollar on its round-trip journey to state capitals. So intense have become the differences of opinion over this issue that a leading legislator in one of the states wrote to a group of presidents:

> It is essential that we go beyond our traditional at-distance distrust and vilification to face-to-face effort at engagement, dialogue and trust building.

Obviously, a positive approach to "engagement, dialogue, and trust building" is to remind the parties at dispute of what it is they are seeking to accomplish. The beginning point is to try to determine the aims and functions of the organization to be governed. It has been found that a description of the premises utilized by participants in the dialogue often can lead to more constructive outcomes.

Lifelong Education and Issues of Control

In concepts of lifelong education we find principles to direct our approach to issues of control, as R. H. Dave explains:

> Education is viewed as a continuing process guided by the over-riding goal of improving the quality of life. It takes place in many different complementary forms, of a sequential as well as of a parallel nature. The individual is always at the hub of this process. All other components of the educational action should combine to develop his capacity for self-learning.

> Serious questions have been raised by educators, economists, politicians and others regarding the quality, adequacy and relevance of the present system of education . . . Criticisms have been leveled against the present system because it isolates the school from the home and community, and thus has an alienating influence on the learners. The system is inflexible, too formal, and often found to be dysfunctional when viewed in the context of community needs or new developments.[1]

In these paragraphs there are ideas that carry implications for governance systems. The goal is that of an individual with capacity for self-learning that will help the person to improve the quality of his or her life. The process is a continuing one; various components in the community participate in a complementary relationship. The fact of change is acknowledged—change which requires flexibility to meet community needs. Many inferences can be drawn from these principles of lifelong education and those found in other sections of this book. The following suggest the effect of application of such principles to the process of governance:

> *Integration of school and place of work, and of learning and doing.* Education will necessarily become decentralized into "units of limited size enjoying functional autonomy." Otherwise initiative and change will be stifled by the inertia of large, bureaucratic structures. However, elements of centralized "quality control" will remain.

> *Decentralization.* The administrative and decision-making apparatus of lifelong education would be largely decentralized because decentralization of the greatest possible number of decisions is indispensable in a system founded on responsible choice, on individualization and education defined as "learning" rather than "teaching."[2]

In a similar fashion we can take other elements of lifelong education and trace the meaning for both the appropriate place where certain kinds of decisions can be made and the personnel who would participate in that process. However, at this point our concern is not with something as broad as lifelong education in general. We are examining the community college in its vanguard role in the evolving policy making for lifelong education. From a review of preceding chapters, statements can be made now about community colleges that carry decided implications for questions of governance. Following are some appropriate descriptors.

Descriptors of Community Colleges

- The modifying word "community" is achieving greater recognition and importance.
- To increase community awareness is a high priority objective.
- The institutions are not the same. They serve unique communities and needs.
- The institution must be able to change as communities change with new conditions, demands, and circumstances.
- The mission of the community college is to encourage and facilitate lifelong education with community as process and product.

- The college affirms that there is no better way to develop viable communities than to involve the citizens, as many as possible, in learning experiences where they can interact.
- The college emphasizes community development—establishing linkages and launching cooperative ventures with other community institutions.
- The college is based upon the belief that local communities are capable of identifying and addressing their own problems.
- It is a primary function of community colleges to aid those in the community who want to learn how to secure certain basic necessities, among them: housing, health, employment, food, and citizenship rights and responsibilities.
- The college assists in developing the capacities of citizens to be self-reliant, self-supporting, and able to contribute for as long as possible.
- The college has on-going, continuing relationships with participants who are broadly dissimilar in age, motivations, abilities, and interests.
- Priority is given to those whose educational options are limited by a variety of circumstances.
- The college collaborates with other community agencies to define the clientele, shape programs, and provide access.
- The college seeks to be part of an integrated system of community services.
- The college encourages working relationships among other institutions and agencies having shared concerns for community and individual development.
- The college relates on a regular basis with people in business, industry, the labor unions, and agriculture, as well as others.
- The college is uniquely qualified to become the *nexus* of a community learning system.

What Meaning for Governance?

If we were to design a governance system for institutions with these characteristics and were primarily concerned with determination of areas of local control vis-a-vis state control, what features would deserve particular attention?

Community orientation is certainly a paramount factor. And we note that communities are different and that they change. State policy would need to take into account these differences and provide opportunity, and perhaps even incentives, for the institutions to change as warranted. It is understood that the institutions are capable of collaborating with other agencies to identify and address problems in the community. It is also acknowledged that they engage in a similar process in identification of clientele, in providing access, and in shaping programs. As will be evidenced below, we are approaching here what might be termed "state space." In matters of access and particular clientele, the state demonstrates a clear interest. It is at this point that the state and local district have shared authority and responsibility.

In further examining the descriptive statements, we note that community development and the goal of "viable" communities with citizen involvement are highlighted. There is reference to cooperative endeavors and programs that transcend age, motivations, and interests. Both the capacities of individuals to be self-reliant and productive and similar collective qualities of the citizenry are seen as objectives of the learning process. Would all of this not suggest that provisions for control should encourage substantial decision making responsibility and authority at the community levels? If not, how does the citizenry develop such capabilities? A college focused on community development would in its own operations provide opportunity for developmental experiences on the part of the community. The product is achieved through involvement in the process.

Above all else, continuing capability in an institution to determine what its appropriate and desired mission will be is needed to assure that both local and state interests are met.

Earlier we said that it is not feasible at the national level and perhaps not at the state level to have a precise, specific description of community college mission. Community differences preclude that, and the pace of change adds to the complexity of the problem. Further, mission determination must be a continuing process in the individual institution. It is not a one time only proposition. What is needed at the state level, therefore, is establishment of conditions that help institutions become capable of determining suitable actions within broad policy guidelines. Of greatest concern to those interested in fostering appropriate learning opportunities should be that of the continuing viability of the organization rather than a catalogue of its services. To monitor "viability" is a much more difficult task than to review courses, programs, budgets, and proposed building plans. If it is not done sensitively, then the state procedures themselves will tend to obscure the search. But surely ways can be determined to observe and report the vital signs. Only then can there be assurance that state funds are effectively utilized. Program reports will not provide such assurance. Perhaps community impact studies would be useful in this regard. Certainly it is in the outcomes of the educational process that the quality of the institution should be revealed.

Qualities That Give Vitality

If the state legislative and regulatory framework is to encourage the development of institutional capabilities, the following are characteristics to be nurtured. They were cited earlier. Now they are considered in terms of their implications for control:

1. The college is adaptable. It is capable of change in response to new conditions and demands, or circumstances.
2. The college operates with a continuing awareness of its community.
3. The college has continuing relationships with the learner.
4. The college extends opportunity to the "unserved."
5. The college accommodates to diversity.
6. The college has a *nexus* function in the community's learning system.

With this picture of the community college as it is influenced by the concepts of lifelong education, we have briefly considered implications for dealing with issues of control. We can now examine in a more detailed way developments in communities and states to ascertain where the strains exist in the tug-of-war between state and community over who calls the shots in the evolving community college.

Somewhat of a Dilemma

There is really little question about the direction of community college interests. They are directed toward the community. An institution, uncertain some years ago whether it was higher or secondary education and where it belonged in the scheme of things, has by and large acknowledged that the community gives it reason for being.

143

The colleges describe themselves as community-based—they utilize space and personnel throughout their districts, and derive programs from community needs and interests. Most of them have established large numbers of cooperative arrangements with other community agencies and institutions. The frequency of interaction increases among college personnel and those in other community organizations. Citizens are involved in forums for identification and discussion of community issues. Taken quite seriously is the suggestion that community development becomes a major objective of this kind of college. An experienced observer would undoubtedly report that, beyond any period in its history, the community college is close to being exactly that—the community's college.

However, a predicament looms on the horizon. In fact, it is even closer at hand. During the past few years a sharp increase in the proportion of financial support received from state levels has been accompanied by state-level monitoring, auditing, and decisions that affect the programs and operations of the colleges. It is reported that the time span between identified need and response becomes longer, that initiatives and creativity are discouraged under the mounting weight of regulations. It is also reported that at the same time, as community relationships have increased in importance and frequency, institutional representatives find it imperative to spend more time in the state capital "protecting their interests." Some may claim that this is an overstatement of the situation. It may be, in some cases, but in general the mood among college representatives is one of frustration at now having two "masters." Moreover, there is the added concern that the state, inappropriately, has its hands in matters that can better be determined locally. Regardless of whether the charges in all respects are warranted, the fact is there is mounting tension between those responsible for the institution at local and state levels. The flow of college interest in the direction of community, and the tendency for the state to exercise more authority over college operations, contains a disruptive rip tide.

View from the State

One of the questions heard in state capitals is whether, in light of changing conditions in the communities, local boards of trustees are capable of governing the colleges. Will they stand up against power blocs or will they become representative of community interests that tend to become divisive? Concerns are expressed about local boards and collective bargaining, and whether "they will give away the store." Will commitments be made which require either more appropriations or funds earmarked for specific purposes (such as faculty salaries)?

A member of a state board for community colleges charged that at both state and local levels there appeared to be erosion in credibility of board members:

> Instead of the board members, people presumably without vested interests, serving as credible buffers, the institutions are right up against the legislature. A board member ought to be able to say to the state legislature, look, I'm not getting a dime for this and members of the legislature ought to listen. The administrator may have a stake in this, the faculty members, and even the students do, but I don't, and the legislator should listen. But the boards at both local and state levels are weak in the sense of their being visible and being credible.

It has already been reported in the section on finance that a legislative analyst was of the opinion that community colleges do not review their budgets as strictly as do state offices. A state-level official echoed that view and added that it was the impression in the state capital that some districts are well managed, others not.

Was the action authorized in the Budget Act of July 6, 1978, in California an indication of concern by the legislature and governor as to whether local trustees would safeguard equity for sectors of the California citizenry? This is what happened. The California community colleges are governed by local boards of trustees. When property tax revenues were cut back as a result of Proposition 13, however, new and massive state appropriations were required. State officials apparently considered it necessary to assist local boards to identify priorities because certain programs were mandated. Districts were required to maintain, during 1978-79, a proportionate level of service (85 percent of 1977-78 funding) in nearly a dozen programs. Included were: elementary and secondary basic skills in mathematics, history, government, and language arts; English as a second language; citizenship for immigrants; programs for substantially handicapped persons; programs for apprenticeship; and short-term vocational programs with high employment potential.

What was the meaning of the mandate? Did state action imply that these programs would not have been part of the community college mission if locally determined? Or, were advocates for these constituencies at the state level politically powerful and not inclined to take a chance on local determinations? Whatever was responsible, the incident is an example of state authority determining programs in locally governed institutions.

State officials say that, with new circumstances, new relationships will have to be worked out, declaring it is not their intent to tell the colleges specifically what to do. In a letter to a community college district, the chairman of a subcommittee on education in the state legislature expressed his conviction that there is necessitated an appropriate sharing of power and authority; moreover, he was emphatic in stating that the legislature had an interest it must maintain:

> Since we have a shared authority and responsibility pursuant to the people of this state and their constitution, we need to work out, likely on an on-going, negotiated issue by issue basis, how we are going to share our power and control. The legislature is unlikely, for example, ever to abolish the education code prohibition against racism and sexism and leave that to local control. Nor would we try to establish curriculum locally course by course.

How It Looks from the Community

That suggestion of "issue by issue negotiation" worries many community college people. "Shouldn't we get our directions from the community rather than from the state legislature?", they ask. When I informed a group of trustees from several community colleges that I was looking for perceptions of essential elements in the mission of community colleges and that my primary contacts were with state-level policy makers and legislators, I was informed immediately that my approach was wrong:

> Looking at the legislature is looking in the wrong direction. It is the trustees who are concerned about what the taxpayers want or need. It is the taxpayer who, regardless of age, says I want something for my dollar. Of course, what he wants and what he is willing to pay for might be two different things.

Another group of trustees resented the necessity to get permission of the state house and senate before they could move forward with a local tax election for the college. It was their opinion that local boards are fully capable of governing their institutions and that state personnel give no evidence of having a corner on wisdom.

There are state personnel who concur in that assessment. For example, fiscal analysts intimated that they probably were the only staff in the state capital to believe that it is dangerous for that level of government to take a role in determining programs in community colleges. They tended to see financing as a partnership, expressing the hope that state direction would not be dictatorial:

> As the governmental structures become more directive, the response time of the institution very likely will increase, so community ought to be the big word and the college has to be responsive. But it won't be if you centralize control and policy. If you do centralize, there is another effect, you begin to find everything looking alike, although the communities are different.

Concerns are expressed about the mounting flow of information from institutions to the state. Reporting requirements multiply. A state-level expert in the field of lifelong education, whose responsibilities are broader than community colleges, declared that the "heavy hand of bureaucracy" discouraged institutional initiatives. She gave examples of how what she viewed as promising ventures were smothered because of "bureaucratic requirements."

And, said a community college president, "We seem to be less adaptable than the aborigines. We are moving into an era of central control and the farther you get from the pump, the more difficult it is to carry water in your hands."

What accounts for this apparent erosion of local control? Is the answer only to be found in the larger fiscal role played by the state? Additional reasons were cited by an authority on public policy who knew his state very well. The state, he observed, is used as an appeals court for aggrieved local people. The legislature is used in this way by faculty, administrators, students, and even trustees. In his estimation, this unfortunate situation can be blamed on local people who take campus or community problems to the state rather than on "power-hungry" officials. He added:

> If we are to maintain a sense of local initiative we need to work out our grievances at the local level. We need to maintain a sense at the campus level of fate over our institutions. The legislature has become the appeals court and the boards are squeezed out of the process.

A disinclination to work out matters at the local level was evidenced by state association representatives who testified before the Board of Governors of the California Community Colleges on a proposed funding measure. Spokesmen for the teachers association, after raising numerous questions about faculty involvement and benefits, declared that the level of trust is poor in the districts. There is need for sanctions which can be imposed by a state-level mechanism. Further, he asserted, there should be provisions for a state-level body to evaluate districts. A person representing alumni of the students association noted that the document under consideration placed major accountability for the institutions in the hands of local boards. He strongly urged that this arrangement be supplanted by a stronger state board of governors and chancellor's office. He proposed a requirement that local boards make all documents available to the chancellor's staff or be penalized by the withholding of state appropriations.

An observer imbued with the philosophy of community-oriented institutions and the values of local decision making confesses some amazement at the positions taken by faculty and former students of institutions charged with leadership in community lifelong education. The plaintive assertion, "our institutions are not well understood," may refer to those within the gates as well as those on the outside. A state board member wondered about that:

> The big question is: can we get our act together? There are divisive forces and these forces become more divisive under pressures of economy. The English teachers versus vocational teachers. Full-time faculty versus part-time faculty. Faculty versus administrators. I don't know whether we can do it. The challenge is now in our ball park.

Time for Proposals

Others agree that it is time for community college leadership to come forward with their proposals. To merely dissent and express concern is a limited and nonproductive approach to problem solving. Without question, the old familiar ways of doing things are gone. Circumstances have changed and will continue to do so. Foremost among our aims now is the establishment of policy environment and regulatory practice that will facilitate the operations of the institutions to fulfill their promise as colleges for the community. Obviously with regard to control, it is neither all local or all state. Basically, at question is the suitable proportion of each authority that must obtain. An educator at the state level suggests that there is "a lot of rhetoric about local *versus* state control":

> This doesn't mean that the community colleges have to be run from the state level. It would be a good idea to get people to cool the

rhetoric. The thing we need to work at is how to avoid clogging up the system of bureaucracy. There has been shared control in the past. One of the basic questions that is going to be asked repeatedly now is: What about equity? What interests need to be determined at the local level if people are well served? The community college people need to come up with proposals.

What kinds of questions are legislators and state-level officials "entitled" to ask? In light of the characteristics which have been given of "viable" community colleges, which of the following represent valid areas of state-level interest? These are among the questions which emerged out of interviews in several states:

Questions by State Authorities

- What are community colleges doing?
- What should be state priorities in funding community colleges?
- Should the state ratify the changes that have taken place in community college programs and services?
- Can we continue to fund at an adequate level community colleges that have taken on such awesome responsibilities?
- Can we afford to implement that ideal—every American has the right to education?
- What are the cost benefits of adult and continuing education?
- How do we prioritize the state's limited resources?
- What will it cost?
- Is the educational community exercising prudence in utilization of the taxpayer's funds?
- What is the state's interest in community colleges?
- How can we consolidate and reallocate resources? With public school enrollments going down, why should there not be a decline in the number of community college students?
- How well are students in community colleges prepared for transfer to four-year colleges and universities?
- Should high school completers who have not scored well on the public school minimal competency test be eligible for admission to community colleges?
- Should a competency test be utilized in community colleges before the associate degree is conferred?
- Do citizens of this state have a *right* to minimal competency?
- Can remedial services be justified in terms of costs to the taxpayers?

- Is there a widening educational gap between the "haves" and the "have-nots"?
- Should the state pay for recreational types of programs, arts, and crafts?
- What is the state's benefit in non-degree oriented activities?
- What is an appropriate division of labor among the public postsecondary institutions of the state?
- How do we reduce competition for funds among educational institutions?
- What assurance do we have that the institutions are well-managed and state funds utilized for the purposes intended?

It would be an interesting experience to bring together legislators, fiscal analysts, heads of coordinating boards, budget officers, state education agency heads, and trustees at local and state levels, as well as community college presidents, to tackle an agenda with those questions as a point of beginning. The focal point would be, "Whose business is this?" or "to what degree is this our business?", not an attempt to answer each question.

Creating a Framework

We can consider these four questions as a starting point: What is the single most important process/product of the community college, from the point of view of (1) the learner, (2) the local community, (3) the state government, and (4) the federal government?

The answers reveal the central values held for the community college and these values will order our policy priorities. For example, Americans hold to the value that the most fundamental federal policy in education is equality of opportunity. The next question, then, is whether actual practice reflects the policy priority. Federal policy is expressed primarily by the large dollar flow into need-based student aid programs, particularly the Basic Educational Opportunity Grants provided by law.

But the existing practices in student aid are not achieving equality of opportunity in the colleges. We know that the students often are those with limited options; they have little time and money to invest in learning. These are learners who may enroll half-time or less than half-time. They are also independent students with family responsibilities. Yet federal guidelines severely limit dollar aid to the independent, or half or less than half-time student. Federal education policy directed toward equality of opportunity could be more effectively realized if changes were made in the student aid programs to better reflect needs.

What are the implications? If equal opportunity means, first of all, access to basic fundamental learning, then community colleges are challenged to deliver remedial and developmental programs which meet federal expectations. By the same token, however, the federal government has a responsibility to provide adequate support for this learning need.

It could be achieved by shifting the flow of BEOG funds from baccalaureate oriented students to remedial students (assuming constant dollars) or an increase in total federal dollars granted to education. It would require a readjustment of college financial aid officers' orientation from the young full-time to the older part-time students.

This is a political question based in expectations for social justice. It must be resolved in at least two places. First, the community college will need to consider its mission—and how remedial education does or does not comprise part of its mission. Second, the federal and state governments need to consider, through the political processes, the priority they place on remedial learning—and the level of support they will provide.

There will be a need for clear understanding of who will assess need, who sets political priorities, who pays the bill, who provides learning services, and who measures results. Such responsibilities must be spelled out in the new policy framework.

The troublesome obstacle is that the new policy framework is likely to be more complex than are the existing frameworks. Because priorities may be established and supported in several "spheres" simultaneously, the answers to those questions in the paragraph above will be a complex grid. Finance and governance may be more layered, or more disaggregated, than in previous decades. Delivery and evaluation will likely also be far more complex. But these may be the precise strengths of our institutions as they face an exponentially increasing rate of change. A mechanism to continually adjust the fabric of the community college—by integrating need, priority, social politics, money, governance and accountability into one framework—presents our most immediate challenge and potential as organizations for lifelong education.

Local Initiatives

Wherever the locus of power, the ability of community colleges to take initiatives and to act quickly has been found significant in a number of studies. In its report, *More than Survival*, the Carnegie Foundation for the Advancement of Teaching saw a brighter future for community colleges than for many other institutions and attributed that fact, at least in part, to its adaptive qualities:

> Public community colleges have substantial growth prospects but also their sense of realism and their sensitivity to external changes contrast sharply with that demonstrated by many institutions in other categories.

Similar research-based views were expressed by Dorothy Knoell in one of her studies of California community colleges. She attributed the strength of the institutions to:

> . . . their ability to respond individually and collectively to state and local needs for new programs and services rather quickly, often without the infusion of new special funds . . . The findings of the study tended to confirm the wisdom of state policy giving as much autonomy to the community colleges as possible. The communities which the colleges serve differ widely with respect to the present and potential student clienteles, availability of other opportunity for postsecondary education, and feelings about what their college ought to be and do.[3]

If those studies were made today would they still reveal the ability to be quickly responsive? A substantial body of opinion would say no. Changes in financial patterns over the past few years coupled with increase in the assumed inevitable state requirements may be seriously blunting the initiative-taking capabilities of these community institutions. A critical point has been reached—not just in terms of what the community college is now but for what it can become—as it plays its part in lifelong education for the community. At the risk of appearing to be overly dramatic, the picture which comes to one's mind, in response to comments by community college personnel, is that of many people laboring like Lilliputians to tie the 1000 little cords that, put together, bind the giant—to make powerless a social institution created to free people. Obviously, state officials don't "buy" that.

How then can the proper balance of power be achieved? In the words of a conscientious state-level budget officer, how can there be established that "fine line between state policy which follows broad principles, and procedures which dictate applications and likely preclude the capacity for modification and making things relevant."

It is not enough to tinker with the mechanism of institutional control. One could emphasize the need for strong local boards and point out that people of quality will be interested only if state policy encourages meaningful activity. Other suggestions come to mind; for example, the need for a strong, well-equipped, technically proficient staff at the state level to provide information to policy makers that describes what community colleges are doing that benefits the state. But such suggestions do not match the urgent requirements confronting us. Questions of control can be answered satisfactorily only in terms of aims, objectives, and goals of the institutions and of the state. Priorities and policies have their rootage in goals. Before questions of decision making and authority can be dealt with effectively, we must talk about goals. We must return to the "premises."

Goals of Another Time

Twenty years ago there was a generally accepted goal for education in this country. It went something like this: "Every individual shall have opportunity for appropriate education up to the maximum of his potential." At that time there was great concern about the ability of postsecondary education to adapt to the needs of the "on-coming tide of students." Guiding that adaptation were state master plans for higher education formulated in the early and mid-fifties. Taken into account were new circumstances in the environment. Among these was the approach of a "college-age" population bulge, plus heightened educational aspirations for millions of veterans made possible by the GI Bill. It became clear that enrollments could double. It also became clear that the solution was not to be found by building new state colleges in every legislator's district. Thus, statewide educational opportunities were envisioned through systems of universities, colleges, and community colleges. According to plan, some functions were decentralized and others centralized. Although there has been criticism of the planning and coordinative arrangements that were developed, by and large they have worked well up to this point. A massive expansion of the educational capabilities of the nation took place—and educational opportunity was extended and diversified.

The primary objective in planning 20 years ago was to increase capacity for the traditional college-age population. During the next two decades, unlooked-for developments transformed institutions whose initial preoccupation was to deal effectively with larger numbers of students. The profound socio-economic events in our nation during the 1960's and 1970's entered the institutions in the persons of our students and demanded change in those institutions. Much more resulted than increased capacity. Many educational institutions adapted in impressive ways to the needs and interests of an ever-widening spectrum of the total population. Now that movement confronts a perceived limitation of financial means at the same time that the environment provides new challenges. Limitations understandably call for priorities. And priorities raise questions of values. Values require reference points, bench marks, a sense of direction. It is possible that the greatest danger we face in the field of education is decision making without agreement upon a sense of direction. How do we get a sense of direction?

Need for New State Studies

It is time for a thorough review of educational services and needs in terms of the significant changes occurring in our society that have implications for the education sector. I have referred to many of those changes. Studies should begin with assessment of educational needs at the community level and involve broad participation of the citizenry. The concept of lifelong education should serve as the major guiding principle for reviewing the educational systems. Such participation has a number of advantages—understanding among taxpayers and voters may be increased and discussions will likely be realistic and concrete.

Earlier there was reference to education sector planning. The approach "goes far beyond the traditional boundaries of formal education; it encompasses training and resource development in other sectors such as agriculture, industry, health, nutrition and public services. . . . it is not a relatively self-contained system. It has multiple intersections with almost every facet of national development."[4]

"Intersections" need to be explored. Some of these are between different kinds and levels of educational institutions. There has already been reference to the large numbers of adults served by the public schools. The community school movement with its dedication to lifelong learning opportunities continues to expand. Although the walls perhaps are not tumbling down, those that separate schools and colleges are beginning to erode.

The office of educational credit of the American Council on Education works with industrial and business organizations and trade unions to devise ways of translating education and training to those organizations into academic currency.

Willard Wirtz calls for bridges between what have been the almost totally separate worlds of education and of work, both to enrich the human experience and to increase the value of the economy's one "boundless resource"—the creativity of its people.

Expectations for the Studies

In the studies and discussions there will need to be recognition that non-formal learning and training is of equal importance to formal education, and that distinctions between the two will be increasingly difficult to make. Informal education includes such learning as formal training on-the-job, apprenticeship, adult education (an archaic term), and, in the words of Harbison, "the entire range of learning processes and experiences outside the regular graded school system." Obviously, interaction will need to occur between and among people who may not have conversed before. A fine perceptive quality will be required of leaders in education to see the opportunities that exist and the ability to develop working relationships with those organizations that have planning and operational responsibilities for varied social and economic functions. Here's what we would expect to come out of these studies:

1. A better and wider understanding of the rapidly changing characteristics of educational consumers and how their numbers sharply increase upon response to their needs and interests.

2. An awareness of the diversity of institutions providing educational services. By and large, college and university education in the past has been perceived as though it were the beginning and the end—a monopolistic, monolithic structure with power obtained through its credentialing functions. It is a pyramidal form, with the graduate school at the sharpened apex modifying and influencing all that is below it as the structure broadens to include larger and larger numbers. By implication those persons who have not reached the summit have been less than successful. A look at actuality today will show that the perceived monolith no longer has credence. Sixty million adults pursue learning activities important to their lives.

3. A statement of goals and perspectives. Where do we look for this statement? I propose new initiatives at local, institutional, state, and regional levels to work out our educational goals and perspectives. Perhaps the very *process* of bringing together diversified

citizenry to examine education and the way we live will be of equal importance to the conclusion reached. Theodore Wertime charged that a "malaise" that destroyed Rome and now threatens the United States derives from the ever greater administrative complexity of urban society. He asks whether civilized states could have been organized differently than they were.

> Could they somehow have achieved an ecumenical and dynamic existence without the centralized establishments of wealth, power and written learning? , , , Must institutions of power inevitably become centralized, ossified and, in Toynbee's words, grotesque?[5]

4. A proposed policy framework to encourage desirable diversity and institutional initiatives and adapatability. Educational needs are manifold and they keep changing. Even at their best, institutions tend to become ponderous in their ability to act, but conditions can be designed to facilitate initiatives, to maintain agility. Some state-level policy makers fear that institutional ambitions will get out of hand if the colleges are given "their head." Although these possibilities are acknowledged, the greater threat is that of suffocation of creativity and thrust under multiplying layers of administrative hierarchy between the scene of action and the locus of the decision that triggers institutional behavior. Furthermore, in our search for answers to coordination and a basis for resource allocation, we have often developed categories and classifications into which institutional behavior must be pressed, trimmed, and pounded for a satisfactory fit. As stated earlier, heavy reliance upon the academic credit system serves as an example of the restrictive climate.

The future is full of unknowns. Many of the old rules for making projections and for planning seem no longer to apply. The voice of the authority in a given field is heard with skepticism; in fact the voice often speaks with equivocation. A variable like the tripling of oil prices can have the well-known domino effect on educational institutions. Nevertheless, we must plan. The institution that can deal with the uncertainties before us is the one that has a "sensing" capacity, a system of intelligence that detects significant changes in the environment and analyzes these for their meaning to the institution. Equally essential, the institution must be able to adapt, to initiate change in the institution, to be free to act.

5. Alternative ways of demonstrating accountability. Rather than being defensive in the face of pressures for accountability, we should take initiatives in devising accountability measures that free

the institution for its most effective performance. These would surely include the assurance that each institution have a set of objectives which serve two purposes: Before the fact, they provide the basis for resource allocation; after the fact, they provide the basis for evaluation. The need for measures of performance in terms of institutional objectives has never been more apparent. "Value added" is a concept of promise whose development is still before us. Another approach to accountability is through the educational audit which is transmitted to the institution's board of trustees. The audit is based upon the notion that the most significant output of an educational institution is made up of the skills, knowledge, appreciations, and attitudes learned by students. Other measures include follow-up studies of students in relation to their "intents" or objectives.

6. Encouragement of voluntary coordination among institutions with common interests. Mandated missions often result in a kind of grudging compliance. There may be a consequent absence of alertness to environmental changes and new opportunities for service. Is it not possible that the same bodies that mandate mission, role, and scope could devise incentives to attract institutions to areas of educational need appropriate to their objectives? And further, would it not be possible also to establish a system to reward voluntary efforts toward coordination and cooperation? What is needed is a process by which institutions will acknowledge common interests and seek an approach to a given need which will best meet that need and economize upon the resources available. The network of relationships will include institutions beyond the conventional educational family, e.g., departments of recreation and parks, public libraries, and city and state planning authorities. Broad areas of mission will need to be stipulated at state levels, but precise and specific assignments and proscriptions will become more impractical as life and learning are perceived as flowing in one stream. Implementing measures, including funding, are needed to encourage continuous assessment of educational needs, cooperative planning, and institutional initiatives toward provision of services.

New Structures for New Times

To sound the reprise, change is occurring in American education. Change which is wholesome and promising. Successful learning experiences are leading people toward other unknowns to be probed, at ascending levels of complexity and challenge. This new spirit of learning requires new descriptors, a new terminology, an adaptive structure. Indeed, a significant contributing factor to the trauma some institutions experience in the face of financial constraints may be the limited moves to date to shape the institutions and their policy framework to the new realities. Issues of authority and control can be resolved only by a broadened understanding of that new educational land into which change has led us.

[1] R. H. Dave. *Foundations of Lifelong Education*. Paris: UNESCO, 1976.

[2] Ibid.

[3] Dorothy M. Knoell. "Challenging the 'Model and the Myth.'" *Community and Junior College Journal* 47: 22; November 1976.

[4] Frederick H. Harbison. *Education Sector Planning for Development of Nation-Wide Learning Systems*. OLC Paper No. 2. Washington, D.C.: American Council on Education, 1973.

[5] Theodore A. Wertime. "The Aging of America." *The Washington Post*, January 1, 1976, p. A15.

Chapter VIII

LEADERSHIP

How to we get from here to there? What will it take to bring about community colleges based upon the concepts presented in the first four chapters of this book? There are difficult hurdles to be cleared. For example, differences are evident between the views proposed and perceptions of state legislators and other state officials. Those views are of more than academic interest because they translate into funding patterns which have a great deal to do with the programs and services of the institution. And a third domino in that set is the college control apparatus, which characteristically has a close relationship with money sources. Furthermore, problems exist closer to home, in the institutions themselves. Differences of opinion exist among faculty, and trustees as well, about directions in which the institutions should be moving. The recommended changes will depend on people who can point the way, make the case, affect change, and marshal public support. Leadership of the highest order is required.

Where Are We Going?

In moving people toward an objective, the beginning point is to make that objective visible in ways that persuade shared effort toward its achievement. The essential element in leadership is to give visibility to the objective and to indicate the direction to those who will participate in the enterprise. Implicit in all of this is the notion that the leadership itself is clear on what it wants to achieve. Some observers and community college personnel themselves doubt whether that can be assumed. "We still have public support and confidence," declared a state board member. "The big question is what do we want to be?" And more specifically, "What is it that the people in the institutions and their constituencies do not want to give up when the resources are limited and priorities must be established?"

A former trustee saw these kinds of questions as central. And they were not being answered. "The heaviest responsibility that we bear now," he said, "is some thought about where we are going. Administrators are not being trained to think about educational issues. We need leadership."

Long associated with community colleges, he described his views as somewhat pessimistic. It was his reluctant opinion that over the next five to 10 years, community college developments will be determined to a great extent by people outside of the movement largely because those in the movement do not have a strong philosophical dynamic.

> Ten years ago we seemed to be rather clear on what we were up to. Community college people were saying, here's what we ought to build; here's what we ought to do. We want your help. Now many presidents are sitting back resting on their accomplishments and new presidents are coming in who are representative of the manager model. They are not leaders. They are not thinkers. They are good technicians and we're not doing much thinking about where community colleges should go. There is no clear sense of purpose. There is a definite lack of leadership.

That, of course, is one man's opinion, but an informed and sympathetic one. At the college where he was formerly a trustee, they "threw their president off campus one summer, saying to him, 'take your family and go think and read.' They gave him two and one-half months to relax and renew himself. The vice-presidents of the institution were there to take care of the problems. The buildings had been built and now it was time to think."

"The buildings had been built." The Plateau Problem. That phrase may reveal another problem confronting community colleges in their evolutionary process. Said a group of faculty and trustees:

> When a college is new people dive in and get the job done. There is a high level of morale. Then after a few years they seem to want to rest. They get new facilities and then the concerns change. They get concerned about the size of their offices. The institution may reach a plateau. There are other problems of finance and enrollment. There may be developmental stages in an institution's life similar to those in the individual. The question is, how do you get the challenge back into the institution? How do you sharpen the cutting edge?

A trustee concurred in the thought that some institutions gave evidence of pausing at least for a deep breath before moving on:

> At present the community colleges are a cost-based system and each year there is an inflation factor cranked in. So next year will be much the same as last year. What we need is a new intellectual bond issue. We need to get some brain power mobilized to do some better things. What will happen in the next five years? The best that will happen is that we'll stay where we are, but if they drain the pool we're in trouble. Unless we do something to generate some risk-takers, people something like those who originally put the system together, we will not move. Where can we find those entrepreneurs?

How do you sharpen the cutting edge? How do you generate the risk-takers? State-level observers frequently comment on changes now taking place in institutional leadership. Consensus exists on the fact of change, but there are mixed views with regard to the probable results. An association head put it this way:

> The entire leadership corps has changed and the community college guys are not willing now to get together and to pound out their differences. There used to be leaders who had enough charisma and leadership style so people would stay together and get things worked out. Now it's a different breed of people and you cannot perpetuate a sense of commitment.

A state-level official described a similar scene in a slightly different way. He said that the personnel changes are so substantial that you could say they are in the process of moving to a new generation of leadership in his state. Further, he expressed concern that community college personnel as a group are "terribly inbred, much more so than the four-year field." He felt they needed to develop the capability to talk with people who are not hostile toward them but who have a different language and different responsibilities.

Changing an Institution

The community college *is* moving into a new generation. In more than 500 communities 10 to 20 years ago the objective was clear— build a college. They voted taxes. Local boards were selected, a president appointed. He selected a core staff. They developed curricula, administrative procedures, recruited other staff, and located facilities. Students came. Architects were selected and buildings planned. Although there were mud holes on campus and inconveniences and delays were frequent, morale was high. It wasn't always that straightforward and easy, but the objective was plain and understood. We are building a college. That is what we want.

Those were the founding days. With all due credit to the competence and dedication of the founders, the process of changing an institution is often more difficult to nurture and guide than the process of establishing an institution. There are buildings. There are a faculty and board. There are learners. There are policy manuals. There are state level agencies and laws and regulations. Between the founding and adapting periods of community colleges other differences have evolved. Among these are environmental factors such as those referred to previously; the awesome pace of change, austerity in the public sector, increased movement to the state levels by the institutions seeking financial support, other priorities for state and local support, decline in the numbers of traditional college age students, and changes in government characteristics at state and federal levels.

And within the institutions there is student and faculty diversity to be dealt with. In addition, of great importance is the typical phenomenon of institutional momentum—what is done has a strong tendency to persist in style and content.

Opportunities for Leadership

At this point, some people might be inclined to throw up their hands and seek early retirement. Others will perceive unusual opportunities for the exercise of leadership and be grateful that the infrastructure is in place. The latter will be confronted by these kinds of questions: "What do we want to be?" "How do we get a clear sense of purpose?" "How do we generate risk takers?" "How do we get the challenge back?"

Clearly, in its discussion of direction and purpose community college leadership must now go outside itself. Reports are heard, too frequently to be easily dismissed, that community college leaders tend to limit their conversations and their organizational efforts to their own numbers. Sample comments: "They are terribly inbred"; and "The self-contained enclave of educators." Possibly related is that common theme heard in many states, "We are not well understood." How does an educator respond to a statement like that? To deal with the problem, the statement is turned around so that somebody is saying, "I do not understand." Now we have a familiar and legitimate statement for those whose profession is the teaching/ learning process. How would we go to work on that problem in the classroom? We would try to "cause learning." We would utilize all of our professional resources to help that student understand.

A serious and troubling question, however, begins to bubble up into the consciousness. Let us assume that our field is sociology. We can teach a concept in sociology if we understand it, have it clearly in mind, and have teaching skills. Is it possible that part of the problem of lack of understanding can be traced to lack of clarity in our own minds? There is nothing wrong with acknowledging that condition. These are days of somewhat cloudy vision at best. Many of us have feelings about what our institutions should do. We have a sense of commitment to serving certain clientele. We have experience enough to operate our institutions on a regular basis. But press us to give a lucid and convincing picture of the community college we want for tomorrow and we may fall short of even our own aspirations. This really should come as no surprise for it has not been a top priority in our job description in the past. Our expertise has been employed to deal with means more than with ends. Present boards and presidents are made up of people with abilities and attitudes that relate to institutional operations. They are generally preoccupied with administrative processes so that there is little time to do anything more.

Excellent managers are required, no question about that. The community college is a complex institution. An increasing array of factors must be dealt with: the design of management information systems, the use of management information, relations with CETA, data collection and analysis, the requirement to do more with less money. On the other hand, there is need to look analytically at problems and opportunities, to focus on environmental factors as they impinge upon these institutions and to analyze the effects of demographic change. There is need for leadership—to point the way, *and* management, "to have charge of and administer."

We need now to give more attention to "leadership"—but no less attention to management. Now it is critical that state legislators understand the changing community college. Ten to twenty years ago the situation was different. The institution was more conventional and most of the support came from the local community where people saw the college daily and had experiences with it. Formerly it was not so essential that community colleges "make their case" in the state capital. Now there is impressive evidence that unless they do so, state staff become the "philosophers, indicating the way to go." And most important, an institution "engaged in preparing men for a type of society which does not yet exist," must be capable to "determine its appropriate and useful services in given circumstances." Basic to judgments of appropriateness is a strong sense of direction and destination—the essential contribution of those who lead.

To Lead Change

Some time ago, a newspaper story reported that the nation's largest forest products firm, Weyerhauser Company, employs science fiction writer Frank Herbert (author of the famous "Dune" trilogy) as a consultant to help the firm determine the markets of the future. Numerous other companies—U.S. Steel, IBM, and American Airlines—utilize science fiction writers as speakers and consultants as a technique to *expand the thinking* of their executives, according to the article. "Making executives more imaginative and envisioning future markets" are two aims of the science fiction consultants. "By and large companies are still run by accountants with green eyeshades," said one writer, "they need to be lifted out of their rut."[1]

Someone defined a grave as "a rut with both ends kicked out." Community colleges are not ready to be laid to rest but they are confronted with the challenge any institution faces in these times of rapid change—how to avoid becoming obsolete.

At a conference sponsored by the American Association of Community and Junior Colleges, the United Auto Workers, and the

AFL-CIO, Kenneth Brown, president of the Graphic Arts International Union, was asked why the union did not more fully utilize the services of the colleges in their training needs. He replied:

> We found we could not use in-place existing facilities or personnel in the training of our people. Our field is changing fast. To use yesterday's personnel to teach on yesterday's equipment we found to be a disaster. We had to create our own training facility, located near the work place. It has to be relevant. Our people need to be completely retrained at least three times during their working lives. We set up our facilities, equipped them with equipment on consignment from employers, and tapped into our own people's skills to develop materials. We scheduled sessions at convenient times and in convenient locations.

Resistance to Change

There is a real possibility that relative to the pace of change in our society, in areas other than the liberal arts, and perhaps even in some of these, there are community colleges which are becoming obsolescent in teaching methods, equipment and faculty. A manager of a large industrial plant told me, "The equipment provided in our vocational-technical institutions is not up to today's technology. So we find we are having to do our own training. People trained in those institutions are using equipment that's ten years out-of-date."

Educational institutions often exhibit a curious paradox. Established to further the teaching/learning process, they are among the institutions most resistant to change in behavior (learning) themselves. A perceptive observer of the American scene in the early part of this century noted that characteristic. In his autobiography Lincoln Steffens writes about his experience at Harvard:

> One of the accepted convictions I had heard most frequently was that education was the way to cure our evils. I did not believe that. Educated people were the slowest to move toward any change. It seemed to me that education was a hindrance to reform, but maybe our education was bad. Mine was, and thinking back over my school and college courses, I could see that one trouble with our education was that it did not teach us what was not known, nor enough of the unsolved problems of the sciences, of the arts, and of life. It did not aim, apparently, to make us keen with educated, intelligent curiosity about the unknown, not eager to do the undone; it taught most of us

only what was known. It gave us positive knowledge when there was no certain knowledge, and worst of all, when we did not particularly want it. We were not curious as students, and we are not curious enough now as men and women.[2]

R. H Dave, two generations later, reports a similar view. Changes in educational systems proceed more slowly than technological changes. And any really profound change in the educational system "takes considerable time to progress from conceptualization to practical application."[3]

The phrase "changes in the educational systems" is too abstract. What it really means is that changed individual and social behavior is required and it is difficult to bring that about. More specifically:

> A very large corps of educators already exists in the person of teachers, administrators and other educational workers. These people are well-entrenched in society and are extensively trained and practiced in many of the values and customs that have already been described as obstacles. Consequently, lifelong education may be accepted in principle among educators but may be blocked in practice by the inflexibility of the group.[4]

To Keep Faculty Up-to-Date

Dorothy Knoell's research provides further evidence of lag and relates specifically to community colleges. "Changes in faculty and staff have been considerably less than found in the student body during the past several years."[5]

Faculty do not all disagree by any means. Many desire their own learning opportunities:

> We need to gear up our systems to the adult learner. This is different from working with children and most of us have not had that kind of training.

> We have not had this type of training ourselves in order to work with people in developing these skills. (With regard to remediation.)

> We can't just be teaching all the time. We need to be doing something else in order to keep up or we will atrophy.

Administrators concur that there is need for change:

As you look to the future in terms of the half-life of an engineer being about five years, how do you keep faculty up-to-date?

Another problem is that the staff is teaching the way they were teaching twenty years ago.

We need to redefine the work of instructors. Many faculty have been content-oriented. They will need to move toward smaller units and to give more attention to the application of content to situations. Where do they go for that kind of training?

We brought in hordes of people in the 1960's, faculty in great numbers. But now the future calls for different people. Actually we may need more administrators and fewer faculty, perhaps managers with academic skills, faculty who are coordinators, new faculty models.

In light of faculty desire to "keep up" and be "retrained" and a quick second to the motion by adminstrators, what is holding things up? Why is there not more happening?

One deterrent may exist in an element long held as a prime value of community colleges—that they are teaching institutions. They do not engage in research. Does Robert Pirsig's description of the "teaching college" exaggerate the dilemma of a faculty member in the community college?

At a teaching college you teach and you teach and you teach with no time for research, no time for contemplation, no time for participation in outside affairs. Just teach and teach and teach until your mind grows dull and your creativity vanishes and you become an automaton saying the same dull things over and over to endless waves of innocent students who cannot understand why you are so dull, lose respect and fan this respect out into the community.[6]

The effect of that routine in times of moderate change is dismal. In these days of social revolution, the result is disastrous. Here we encounter another paradox. Often one of the first things to be eliminated when the budget tightens is provision for faculty enlightenment, revitalization, and renewal. Another factor is involved in the monotony described so graphically by Pirsig. In addition to the centripetal effect of the unrelieved teaching routine, the transition to continual education from the idea of initial training requires quite a different approach to teaching/learning.

At least in principle, we are tending more and more in the direction of "selflearning." The traditional concepts of pedagogy, or of andragogy, tend to disappear into the background with the development of "mathetics" which according to its promoters is a science of *learning*, as opposed to pedagogy, the science of *teaching*.[7]

Without question sweeping changes are required in institutional arrangements, faculty attitudes, and student expectations if "mathetics" is to be our style.

Job Enrichment

Faculty and administrative personnel alike can benefit from utilization of job enrichment theory which will improve the quality of their participation by providing new approaches to establishing roles and the reorganization of institutional structures. Significant experimentation is under way in business and industrial organizations. Examples can be found in Sweden (Volvo), Japan (SONY), and in the United States (Polaroid Corp., IBM, Procter and Gamble). But little has been done in education. Roger Seager, president of Jamestown Community College, says the lack of experimentation in the academic world can be accounted for by the fact that the professorial role in the university has traditionally been seen as the "good life," replete with broad responsibilities and ample opportunities for self growth and personal reward.

"But," says Seager, "the emergence of the community college and the professorial work-life it offers introduces an entirely new problem and challenge. In contrast to the stereotypic rich and varied life of the graduate school professor, the community college professor typically teaches five courses per semester, does no research, enjoys few opportunities to organize his thoughts through writing and publication, handles large numbers of able and not so able students, and deals with subject matter which seldom challenges or forces his professional growth. He functions in a hierarchy and decision-making system between, but perhaps closer to, the high school model than the university. He seldom serves as a consultant and all too often finds the four walls of his classroom the parameters of his work world. And he does this day after day, semester after semester."

Seager asserts: "That community college professors feel constrained, over-managed, and professionally inhibited seems abundantly clear if one is to make anything at all of the expanding unionism, collective bargaining, formal grievances, disengagement, and sheer monotony, to which the major administrative response has been (to date) increased firmness at the bargaining table.''

Seager proposes broadening the professional role of the faculty member, at least for some who may be interested, to that of professor-broker. ''This is a broad role entailing duties as a market researcher, salesman, organizer, teacher, coordinator, administrator, evaluator. The broker helps potential client groups define their needs, identifies the component parts needed, organizes and coordinates the variables of people, places and things; helps plan and sequence the learning experiences, monitors performance and progress, and assesses the worthwhileness of the outcomes.''

This is one approach to an evident problem. There are others. The aim is to make it possible for faculty to be involved in community-based education so that they can experience community relationships, be motivated toward change, and experience the renewal to be gained from expanding environments. Often the excitement of innovation and development is reserved to those who participate in community service programs and the rest of the college is untouched and uninvolved.

Several presidents in a group spoke of the need for faculty to adapt to new clienteles and new circumstances and wondered aloud how institutions could be more creative. One commented:

> After all, it's not much fun to teach English in the same course year after year. We have some happy faculty in our district. They have responsibilities for developing a new criminal justice workshop and as a result of their creative efforts and their success, they are very much in demand throughout the country. Their morale level is very high.

Another president said, in referring to a large industrial plant just a few miles from the campus, ''I don't have a single faculty member who really knows what's going on over there.'' Granted that the visitor is uninformed about the local situation, he finds it impossible not to ask, at least in his own mind, why doesn't the faculty member ''know what's going on over there?''

New Relationships

The manager of that same large plant told me that he would be glad to work out an arrangement with the college so that faculty could be kept up-to-date on the most modern equipment and could get a feel for what is happening in industry. He doubted that the community college could afford to acquire and update the equipment that was needed to train people to effectively fit the needs of his industry, but he did offer to make places available in the plant to give students hands-on experience while working toward an associate degree.

In many technological fields the rate of change is breathtaking. Educational institutions will be able to keep current only by establishing new relationships with business and industry and the professions. More of the teaching in specialized fields may be done by those who are the practitioners. A great deal of the learning will take place in "clinical" settings. Only in these ways will community colleges be able to respond to the justified skepticism of trade representatives like Kenneth Brown. Such relationships will contribute toward faculty proficiency. The concept of "retraining" is inadequate. Personnel in the educational institutions must find ways to have a continuing involvement in the field of their teaching, whether it is graphic arts, optics, nursing, automotive technology, political science, or data technology. Continuing change requires the relationships to be continuous rather than sporadic. Adaptation must be an ongoing process, not an occasional episode. The concept of "symbiosis" referred to previously illustrates the relationship envisioned between education and other community "organisms" in close association or union, "especially where this is advantageous to both."

Sensitive administrators can help faculty maintain "involvement," not only in the obviously fast-changing technological fields, but also in other areas of human experience where the credibility of those who teach is directly related to what they do in their area of expertise, for example in the humanities:

> Think of the salutory effects it would have on their teaching if faculty members were encouraged to do what their work compels them to do: to write, to paint, to act, to play, or to compose, for example. And think of the price we pay for continuing the tradition of exempting community college teachers from any obligation to do these things.

> Periodically, administrators can provide teachers with opportunities for what might be called "creative disengagements" from parts of their college assignments, allowing them to devote time and energy to such things as local historical societies, museums, or community artists' and writers' groups . . . Who is better poised to work with community groups—from the curious to the incarcerated to the aged—than faculty members in community colleges? Creative dis-

engagement from regular duties to take on exceptional ones is surely a desirable alternative to the cynical detachment that eventually leads faculty members to become realtors, antique dealers, or fast-food franchisers in their moonlight hours.[8]

Where community is seen as process in learning, the arrangements proposed above should be amended. Somehow participation in community and ''what their work compels them to do'' would become a part of ''regular'' duties, not something exceptional.

Community Research

One of the regular and essential activities of the community college, not fully acknowledged in institutional organization or funding patterns, is community research; continuing process of identification of problems, needs, and possibilities in the service area of the college. As stated previously, community colleges cannot exercise their awareness function without scientific investigation and inquiry—that is research. We have been considering ways to bring about change in the institution. Continuing study of the community not only provides information necessary for decision making in the college but it offers remarkably rich and appropriate professional development opportunities for college faculty. Experiences at Rogaland College in Norway suggest the possibilities. Much like a community college, Rogaland, located in Stavanger, has established a foundation for research which is actually operated by the county of Rogaland to further and coordinate research on community conditions. It was established as a result of demand by various institutions in the county for a better organized effort to encourage research, particularly that having to do with various spheres of local life. The foundation works closely with the college, although the foundation board includes people from industry, government, and other sectors. The faculty expertise is utilized in projects of the foundation.

Projects for a recent year included: (1) social consequences of the oil activity in Rogaland; (2) a study of cultural life in the expatriate society in Stavanger and its impact on the local community; and (3) a study of parents' need for knowledge about children.

The foundation is also studying water pollution and community culture.

The research contemplated is not esoteric. It is practically oriented with results applied to a community problem or need. And, in accordance with a central element of community college operations, it will be done in association with other appropriate organizations. It is most important to note that community colleges of the future should not advertise as an evidence of their quality that they are "teaching institutions and do no research." The benefits of community research are at least twofold. It results in useful findings that can help to identify and solve problems, and enlivened faculty and staff.

Faculty as a Resource

There are many ways of "enlivening" faculty and staff. Foremost is the recognition that faculty are a resource in leadership of the institution. In the university setting, the talents of professors are often used to help set the directions of the institution. It is worth interjecting here that, although not inevitable, a casualty of the collective bargaining process may be denial to the institution of thoughtful contributions of "employees." On the other hand, even in colleges where collective bargaining does not exist, the expertise of faculty is not often drawn upon to benefit the institution itself. Beyond what have been described as "mundane things at the opening session of the college," what is being done to elicit contributions from the personnel of the institution? Commented some presidents who were wondering how to interest faculty in retraining possibilities:

> Lots of people don't know what is going on or don't care. How do you get hold of these things with regard to faculty? Maybe we need to bombard them with the realities—that we face a political situation—that there is necessity for reduction in force.

There are perhaps some who "don't care." There are many others who may not know "what is going on." It is extremely unlikely that community colleges will move in the directions indicated here unless faculty have opportunity to participate in the discussions of institutional direction.

New approaches to teaching/learning must come. The collage of faculty member, desk, classroom, students, and textbook represents another period. It is now time to identify the tasks to be performed in meeting a variety of new educational needs and circumstances. Persons with appropriate training will be required for such parts of the teaching/learning process as conveyance of information, evaluation, development of course materials, open laboratory and shop staffing, counseling, assessment, and interpretation of community educational needs, clinical supervision, and the development of learning contracts, and other means toward learning. Not everybody needs to know how to do everything in the teaching/learning process. There is too much to know and the pace of change is too great. Careful and continuing analyses of the tasks to be performed will indicate what and how much people need to know to perform their tasks effectively. The amount of time spent at various locales will depend upon the functions to be performed, the nature of tasks. Evaluation will be in terms of how well the tasks are accomplished.

Rather than drive faculty to change, which is probably impossible anyway, incentives and assistance and renewal must be built into the institutional arrangements so that (a) change and up-grading become a stimulating experience, (b) change is rewarding in terms of salary and status, and (c) it is a source of pride to change. It is a tough and demanding exercise to set this up and make it happen. It demands an educational leadership which is rare and probably not found or understood at many institutions.

And What About the President?

A president, even one who might have feared truly competent staff, will now see that it is to his advantage to promote professional development of those around him or her. It becomes increasingly clear, in the light of the concept of executive liability, that the president's welfare is inseparably connected to the competence of his or her associates. Executives can be held accountable not only for their own acts but for the acts or the omissions of others, court decisions have implied. Of at least equal importance, the beam of the spotlight which focuses upon the president must be broadened to illuminate the many other persons whose contributions are essential if the institution is to do its work well. Moreover, the president cannot effectively perform his indispensable function unless he has highly proficient associates to whom many management responsibilities can be delegated. For it is his or her obligation, beyond anything else, to provide that quality of leadership that gives clarity, lucidity, and intelligibility to the institution's goals so that there can be a common understanding of what it is that the participants of the enterprise are going to do together.

Just as faculty need provisions for "job enrichment," "creative disengagements," and opportunities to "know what's going on over there," so does the president if he is to effectively lead. He needs time to observe the broader environment, to think, to organize his thoughts and express them in writing and speaking. He needs time and resources for planning and for relating to other significant organizations in the community beyond those afforded at civic club luncheons. A committee on change could be organized to assist the chief executive. It would be charged to look continuously, with assistance from relevant fields, at all areas of its activities in order to forecast probable developments and consequent needs.

Leadership and the Board

A board of trustees could benefit from somewhat similar provisions: a committee on change to provide a context and occasion to review college policies and programs in light of developments in the community and beyond; time, to think and to plan, and even to provide "job enrichment" to ward off the enervating tendencies toward routine and detail. There is evidence of a high rate of turnover in board personnel. Some say that serving as a trustee is "not fun anymore." The founding days were those of action and accomplishment when the best citizens could be attracted to board membership. Neither collective bargaining nor severe economic pressures had intruded.

Without question, the agenda for trustees has changed just as everything else about the college and the community has changed. Trustees are not powerless, however. They enjoy the right and obligation to take a stand on the quality of the agenda and the quality of the leadership that they feel is needed. The board is the first group to be addressed by the president as he promotes understanding of the community college. In my interviews, I found trustees deeply interested in what I was doing and particularly in questions about community college mission. The board's role in the transition of the institution toward the concepts of lifelong education is crucial. The president can provide leadership in giving visibility to the objectives and in proposing measures for institutional change. But it is the board that decides through policy and budget making as well as in its selection of chief executive officer whether proposals become fact. One is reminded of an ancient gem of wisdom with regard to the relative relationships of man and God. We can paraphrase it to say that the President proposes. The Board disposes. In our communities and institutions, as measures are considered to broaden and clarify understanding of new opportunities for community colleges, trustee participation is essential.

To Marshal Public Support

How does the community college develop power, the capacity to get things done, to secure the resources it requires for its emerging missions? Much has already been said about the flow of power, decision making, to state and federal levels. To complain about that trend is an ineffective exercise. A better way is to build countervailing forces. Among the most significant of countervailing forces are strong, capable voices at the local level; strong presidents, strong boards, and an identified and committed constituency.

How do resources become available for college use? If the college seeks cooperation and a fair share of the dollars available, how does that come about? We have noted that resources are limited. Therefore choices must be made. Choices are often made in line with a law as old as the history of man—it is called *quid pro quo*, or simply something for something, one thing in return for another.

The process by which resources are allocated is not always logical or on a basis of proclaimed need or even merit. If we want something—what will we give in return? It is not enough for the college to put together a series of courses. But will the businessman feel that the college is really addressing *his* needs? Why does the notion persist that a community college may be prostituting itself if it seeks to respond to community interests?

In his book, *Power in the City*, Frederick Wirt defines the city as "a complex set of transactions, or exchanges, among its citizens . . . Characteristic of each transaction is the exchange by one person or group with another for something material or symbolic that contributes to the safety, income, or respect of each. These interactions might also be conceived as a process of exchange whereby actors seek to satisfy interest by exchanging resources according to some calculus of cost and benefit." Wirt, in his analysis of the transactions in San Francisco, describes decisions that involve major allocations of the community resources, that is, the "politics," which decide how most of the public and private goods and services came to be distributed among the citizens. He maintains the need to "understand the actors, structures, processes, and outcomes in such decisional patterns.

"But whatever the degree of such knowledge (local decisional context)," Wirt comments, "its utility lies in an understanding of how to affect community processes and policies. Such knowledge constitutes one of the major resources augmenting an individual's power in the community, but it is obvious that many have little and few have much of this resource.'"[9]

Community Knowledge—A Resource

Is this "knowledge" which constitutes, in Wirt's words, one of the "major resources," also one of the community college's unique resources? Does not the very placement of the college in interfusing with the community give it an intelligence system, a source of data useful in the process of distribution of "goods and services?" What other institution has the linkages into business and industry, the unions and the neighborhoods through cooperative programs, advisory committees, and in-plant services? Faculty are not just of the college, they are of the community. The learners are taxpayers and citizens, most of them involved in their careers. Some community colleges collect and maintain demographic data in computer banks for other community agencies and organizations. Such information is also available to the college for strategic planning. Consider the "local knowledge" that can be elicited as faculty in economics, political science, sociology, anthropology, and history relate their teaching/learning experiences to the cultures of the community. The product surely can be "an understanding of the actors, structures, processes, and outcomes" of decisional patterns.

I am not proposing that the college itself be a political action organization. I am saying that the community college is not only to inform but to be informed, not only is it to be a purveyor of knowledge but it is to be knowledgeable—not only of the Rift Valley as it slashes its way down the continent of Africa but the valleys that divide the cultures of the college's communities. The college needs the means by which to accomplish its ends. The means are more than dollars, but dollars are required. Resources exist that can be tapped by people in the community. Those resources are limited. Decisions are made. Resources are deployed, allocated, and reallocated. The community college is in an enviable position not only to understand the decision making processes but to influence the "actors."

Not many of our institutions have fully perceived their advantages or organized to benefit from them. A basic change in the stance of the institution is required as well as commitments from a variety of college personnel. A community services director described the approach this way:

One of our jobs is to develop a constituency in the area. The whole attitude of the community needs to be shaped in that direction. When you write to City Hall you get a letter back. There is no letter unanswered because there is a vote involved and there should be this same sense of urgency upon the part of all the people at the community colleges. Too often the attitude has been, if you want it you can come and get it.

Qualities of Presidential Leadership

Should it be expected that a president develop a constituency for the college? Where should his priorities lie in his post as executive officer for an institution that encourages and facilitates learning in the community? What qualities should be looked for in a president of a community college for the 1980's? These are suggested:

1. The President is aware of the dynamics of change in our environment.
2. The President is able to describe persuasively the community college in terms of its functions in facilitating learning in the community.
3. The President has a keen political sense with regard to the environment at both community and state levels and a professional approach to political realities.
4. The President is capable of attracting and nurturing a superior staff and delegating to them such management responsibilities as will free him for leadership tasks.
5. The President relates effectively to the leadership of other major institutions and organizations in the community in such fields as government, health, business, the arts, unions, the media, etc.
6. The President maintains a relationship with his board and state authorities to assure that the college has the capacity to:

   a. be adaptable
   b. be continually aware of its community
   c. relate to learners in a continuing way
   d. extend opportunity to the unserved
   e. accommodate to diversity
   f. serve as a nexus in the community learning system.

A large number of national leaders in the community college field will retire from their executive positions in the next few years. At the same time, community colleges confront new and complex challenges at community, state, and national levels. The shaping of institutions to function in a stream of lifelong education will require leadership on the campuses and in state, regional, and national forums.

Just as Junior College Leadership Centers were established at 10 universities 20 years ago to assist in the development of administrative personnel for that era in community college evolution, again special efforts are required to assist those who seek to qualify for the exacting leadership and management requirements of the changing community college. Particularly needed are experiences to prepare persons who can develop and implement the concept of what the community colleges in the '80's should be. And it is important that they become skillful at interpreting the concept of the community college to others.

Leadership by Community Colleges

We have referred frequently to the stimulating concepts of lifelong education reported by R. H. Dave and his colleagues. They provide well-founded guidance for community college development. And because community colleges already evidence many characteristics that fit the concepts presented, there is a further opportunity and indeed a responsibility for our institutions to assume. Dave says:

> . . . the next step is to implement some of the ideas inherent in lifelong education. If we want to hasten establishment of a comprehensive, unified, flexible and democratic system of education to insure species survival and a higher quality of life, it is necessary to implement theory and practice concurrently. This is a formidable task ahead.[10]

We can "implement some of the ideas." Many of our institutions are doing that. We can "hasten establishment of a comprehensive, unified, flexible and democratic system of education to assure species survival and a higher quality of life." Those are goals to which we have shown our commitment. Community colleges, beyond any other educational institutions of our day, because of what they have already become, can lead in the adoption of lifelong education as a concept for reconstructing educational systems.

I have proposed that in the fall of 1980, 1000 community colleges join with other community organizations to sponsor discussions about the kind of education people need and the policies required to extend learning opportunities throughout life. We have in our institutions and in the Association the capacity and the experience to initiate such discussions—to serve as convenors. We have resources beyond those possessed by other educational institutions to initiate a job that I am convinced must be done.

I urge each community college to begin its own analysis of the local issues surrounding the mission of the community college; to develop materials to create an informed discussion; to build a network of cooperation with other community agencies to plan community forums; and to begin plans for such forums or town meetings or hearings. Whatever the appropriate format, the goal should be the broadest possible involvement of the community in thinking through the mission of the local community college.

And in this process let us see to it that the people in our own institutions are fully involved. Institutions, like individuals, as we have noted, need periodic renewal and revitalization. For an institution to have a sense of mission, the participants require commitment to a set of aims persuasive enough to elicit cooperation and vitality. As threatening to our institutions as the erosion of inflation can be, the greater danger we face is the erosion of our spirit.

It is time for us to consider together—and with those whose influences join ours to shape the community environment—the emerging realities in that environment which set before us tasks and new learning ventures to match the best skills, talents, and leadership qualities that we can bring to them. Above all, we must bring to the job ahead a sense of the values in it, and the vision and vitality needed to get it done.

---

[1] *The Washington Star*, June 17, 1978.

[2] Lincoln Steffens. *The Autobiography of Lincoln Steffens.* New York: Harcourt, Brace, and Company, 1931, p. 644.

[3] R. H. Dave. *Foundations of Lifelong Education.* Paris: UNESCO, 1976.

[4] Ibid.

[5] Dorothy M. Knoell. *Through the Open Door. A Study of Patterns in Enrollment and Performance in California's Community Colleges*. Report No. 76-1. Sacramento: California Postsecondary Education Commission, February 1976.

[6] Robert Pirsig. *Zen and the Art of Motorcycle Maintenance*. New York: William Morrow and Company, 1974.

[7] Edgar Faure. *Learning to Be*. Paris: UNESCO, 1972.

[8] Myron A. Marty. "Work, Jobs, and the Language of the Humanities." *Strengthening Humanities in Community Colleges*. Washington, D.C.: American Association of Community and Junior Colleges, 1980, p. 68.

[9] Frederick Wirt. *Power in the City*. Berkeley: University of California Press, Berkeley, California, 1974.

[10] R. H. Dave. *Foundations of Lifelong Education*. Paris: UNESCO, 1976.

Appendix I

CONCEPT CHARACTERISTICS OF LIFELONG EDUCATION*

1. The three basic terms upon which the *meaning* of the concept is based are *life, lifelong* and *education*. The meaning attached to these terms and the interpretation given to them largely determine the scope and meaning of lifelong education.

2. Education does not terminate at the end of formal schooling but is a *lifelong process*. Lifelong education covers the entire life-span of an individual.

3. Lifelong education is not confined to adult education but it encompasses and unifies all stages of education—pre-primary, primary, secondary and so forth. Thus it seeks to view *education* in its *totality*.

4. Lifelong education includes *formal, non-formal and informal patterns of education*.

5. The *home* plays the first, most subtle and crucial role in initiating the process of lifelong learning. This process continues throughout the entire life-span of an individual through *family learning*.

6. The *community* also plays an important role in the system of lifelong education right from the time the child begins to interact with it. It continues its educative function both in professional and general areas throughout life.

7. *Institutions of education* such as schools, universities and training centres are important, but only as one of the agencies for lifelong education. They no longer enjoy the monopoly of educating the people and can no longer exist in isolation from other educative agencies in their society.

8. Lifelong education seeks continuity and articulation along its vertical or longitudinal dimension. (*Vertical Articulation*)

9. Lifelong education also seeks integration at its horizontal and depth dimensions at every stage in life. (*Horizontal Integration*)

10. Contrary to the elitist form of education, lifelong education is *universal* in character. It represents *democratization of education*.

11. Lifelong education is characterized by its *flexibility* and *diversity* in *content, learning tools* and *techniques*, and *time* of learning.

12. Lifelong education is a *dynamic approach* to education which allows adaptation of materials and media of learning as and when new developments take place.

13. Lifelong education allows *alternative patterns* and forms of acquiring education.

14. Lifelong education has two broad components: *general* and *professional*. These components are not completely different from each other but are *inter-related* and *interactive* in nature.

15. The *adaptive* and *innovative functions* of the individual and society are fulfilled through lifelong education.

16. Lifelong education carries out a *corrective function*: to take care of the shortcomings of the existing system of education.

17. The ultimate goal of lifelong education is to maintain and improve the *quality of life*.

18. There are three major *prerequisites* for lifelong education, namely *opportunity, motivation* and *educability*.

19. Lifelong education is an *organizing principle* for all education.

20. At the *operational level*, lifelong education provides a *total* system of *all* education.

---

*R. H. Dave. *Lifelong Education and School Curriculum*. Hamburg: UNESCO Institute for Education, 1973, pp. 14-25.

Appendix II

ADULT LIFE CYCLE TASKS/
ADULT CONTINUING EDUCATION
PROGRAM RESPONSE*

Developmental Stages	Tasks	Program Response	Outcomes Sought
Leaving Home 18-22	1. Break psychological ties. 2. Choose careers. 3. Enter work.	1. Personal development, assertive training workshops.	1. Strengthened autonomy. 2. Appropriate career decisions.

© 1977 by Vivian Rogers McCoy, Director, Adult Life Resource Center, Division of Continuing Education, University of Kansas.

Reprinted with permission of the Adult Education Association of the United States of America from the October, 1977, issue of Lifelong Education: the Adult Years.

4. Handle peer relationships.
5. Manage home.
6. Manage time.
7. Adjust to life on own.
8. Problem solve.
9. Manage stress accompanying change.

2. Career workshops, values clarification, occupational information.
3. Education/career preparation.
4. Human relations groups.
5. Consumer education/homemaking skills.
6. Time/leisure use workshops.
7. Living alone; successful singles workshops.
8. Creative problem solving workshops.
9. Stress management, biofeedback, relaxation, TM workshops.

3. Successful education/career entry.
4. Effective social interaction.
5. Informed consumer, healthy homelife.
6. Wise use of time.
7. Fulfilled single state, autonomy.
8. Successful problem solving.
9. Successful stress management, personal growth.

Becoming Adult 23-28

1. Select mate.
2. Settle in work, begin career ladder.
3. Parent.
4. Become involved in community.
5. Consume wisely.
6. Homeown.
7. Socially interact.

1. Marriage workshops.
2. Management, advancement training.
3. Parenting workshops.
4. Civic education; volunteer training.
5. Consumer education, financial management training.

1. Successful marriage.
2. Career satisfaction and advancement.
3. Effective parents; healthy offspring.
4. Informed, participating citizen.
5. Sound consumer behavior.

Developmental Stages	Tasks	Program Response	Outcomes Sought
	8. Achieve autonomy. 9. Problem solve. 10. Manage stress accompanying change.	6. Homeowning, maintenance workshops. 7. Human relations groups, TA. 8. Living alone, divorce workshops. 9. Creative problem solving workshops. 10. Stress management, bio-feedback, relaxation, TM workshops.	6. Satisfying home environment. 7. Social skills. 8. Fulfilled single state, autonomy. 9. Successful problem solving. 10. Successful stress management, personal growth.
Catch-30 29-34	1. Search for personal values. 2. Reappraise relationships. 3. Progress in career. 4. Accept growing children. 5. Put down roots, achieve ''permanent'' home. 6. Problem solve. 7. Manage stress accompanying change.	1. Values clarification. 2. Marriage counseling and communication workshops; human relations groups; creative divorce workshops. 3. Career advancement training, job redesign workshops. 4. Parent-child relationship workshops. 5. Consumer education.	1. Examined and owned values. 2. Authentic personal relationships. 3. Career satisfaction, economic reward, a sense of competence and achievement. 4. Growth producing parent-child relationship. 5. Sound consumer behavior

Stage	Tasks	Workshops	Outcomes
		6. Creative problem solving workshops.	6. Successful problem solving.
		7. Stress management, bio-feedback, relaxation, TM workshops.	7. Successful stress management, personal growth.
Midlife Reexamination 35-43	1. Search for meaning. 2. Reassess marriage. 3. Reexamine work. 4. Relate to teenage children. 5. Relate to aging parents 6. Reassess personal priorities and values. 7. Adjust to single life. 8. Problem solve. 9. Manage stress accompanying change.	1. Search for meaning workshops. 2. Marriage workshops. 3. Mid-career workshops. 4. Parenting: focus on raising teen-age children. 5. Relating to aging parents workshops. 6. Value clarification; goal-setting workshops. 7. Living alone, divorce workshops. 8. Creative problem solving workshops. 9. Stress management, bio-feedback, relaxation, TM workshops.	1. Coping with existential anxiety. 2. Satisfying marriages. 3. Appropriate career decisions. 4. Improved parent-child relations. 5. Improved child-parent relations. 6. Autonomous behavior. 7. Fulfilled single state. 8. Successful problem solving. 9. Successful stress management, personal growth.
Restabilization 44-55	1. Adjust to realities of work. 2. Launch children.	1. Personal, vocational counseling, career workshops.	1. Job adjustment. 2. Civil letting go parental authority.

Developmental Stages	Tasks	Program Response	Outcomes Sought
	3. Adjust to empty nest.	2. Parenting education.	3. Exploring new sources of satisfaction.
	4. Become more deeply involved in social life.	3. Marriage, personal counseling workshops.	4. Effective social relations.
	5. Participate actively in community concerns.	4. Human relations groups.	5. Effective citizenship.
	6. Handle increased demands of older parents.	5. Civic and social issues education.	6. Better personal and social adjustment of elderly.
	7. Manage leisure time.	6. Gerontology workshops.	7. Creative use of leisure.
	8. Manage budget to support college-age children and ailing parents.	7. Leisure use workshops.	8. Sound consumer behavior.
	9. Adjust to single state.	8. Financial management workshops.	9. Fulfilled single state.
	10. Problem solve.	9. Workshops on loneliness and aloneness.	10. Successful problem solving.
	11. Manage stress accompanying change.	10. Creative problem solving workshops.	11. Successful stress management, personal growth.
		11. Stress management, biofeedback, relaxation, TM workshops.	
Preparation for Retirement 56-64	1. Adjust to health problems.	1. Programs about nutrition, health.	1. Healthier individuals.
	2. Deepen personal relations.	2. Human relations groups.	2. Effective social skills.
	3. Prepare for retirement.	3. Preretirement workshops.	3. Wise retirement planning.
	4. Expand avocational interests.	4. Art, writing, music courses in performing and appreciation; spon-	4. Satisfaction of aesthetic urge; broadening of knowledge; enjoyment of

Retirement 65+

Tasks	Programs	Goals
5. Finance new leisure.	(continued) sored educational travel.	(continued) travel.
6. Adjust to loss of mate.	5. Money management training.	5. Sound consumer behavior
7. Problem solving.	6. Workshops on aloneness and loneliness, death and dying.	6. Adjustment to loss, fulfilled single state.
8. Manage stress accompanying change.	7. Creative problem solving workshops.	7. Successful problem solving.
	8. Stress management, biofeedback, relaxation, TM workshops.	8. Successful stress management, personal growth.
1. Disengage from paid work.	1, 4, 5, 6. Workshops on retirement, volunteering, aging; conferences on public issues affecting aged.	1, 4, 5, 6. Creative, active, retirement; successful coping with life disengagement; public policies responsive to needs of aged.
2. Reassess finances.	2. Financial management training.	2. Freedom from financial fears.
3. Be concerned with personal health care.	3. Health care programs.	3. Appropriate health care.
4. Search for new achievement outlets.	7. Religious exploration.	7. Help in search of life's meaning, values of past life.
5. Manage leisure time.	8. Workshops on aloneness and loneliness.	8. Fulfilled single state.
6. Adjust to more constant marriage companion.	9. Death and dying workshops.	
7. Search for meaning.		
8. Adjust to single state.		
9. Be reconciled to death.		

Developmental Stages	Tasks	Program Response	Outcomes Sought
	10. Problem solve. 11. Manage stress accompanying change.	10. Creative problem solving workshops. 11. Stress management, biofeedback, relaxation, TM workshops.	9. Philosophic acceptance of death, help in caring for dying and handling of grief. 10. Successful problem solving. 11. Successful stress management, personal growth.

190